WHERE
ON EARTH
IS
GOD
TODAY?

by DESI MAXWELL

Evangelical Publishing Ltd.

First Published in 2007 by Evangelical Publishing Ltd.

Second edition: July 2007

To 'my girls',
Heather, my wife
Rachel and Vicky, daughters.

Preface

This book marks the opening of a whole new chapter in life for my family. Its ublication coincides with the launch of a teaching ministry called XPLORATIONS. For a long time I have been restless to move outside the classroom, where I learned so much preparing lectures. My burden is to take this material to a wider audience. There are so many who are hungry to learn more about the Bible but who cannot come to college for various reasons. My passion is to pass on what others have shared with me in person and in print.

This is a book without footnotes or bibliography. It is not a technical book but more like a map. I hope that it will help you get some bearings on life. I pray that it will clarify where we all fit into God's big plan.

If the map has its shortcomings then they are not the fault of the many folk who have shared the journey with me to date. As a mark of their friendship, some have browsed preliminary copies of this map helping me to clarify my thoughts on paper. To them I say thank you and value their companionship on the uncharted roads that lie ahead.

Desi Maxwell.

Lisburn, 2007

Introduction

What you are holding in your hand is not so much a book as a sort of personal Global Plotting System. G.P.S., as it is popularly called, is now readily available for the motorist, sailor, cyclist and walker. At any given moment the traveller can plot exactly where he or she is on the face of the globe. G.P.S. relates the local to the global, sets the particular in the context of the universal and ensures the individual need never feel lost on the face of the planet.

This little volume is a tentative step toward helping individuals locate themselves in the epic drama of God's plan of redemption. Sadly, too many people have a very limited appreciation of their place in the big picture. Drawing inspiration from the Promise Box, so many survive on 'little thoughts for the day', thereby robbing themselves of the bigger picture. However, our individual experience of salvation is set in the context of a cosmic scheme. The Bible is not merely a reservoir of inspirational thoughts, but rather the revelation of a cosmic plan. 'Jesus and me' only makes sense in the context of God and the cosmos. In these pages we shall try to capture a view from space rather than earth, gaze from the shuttle cockpit rather than through the car windscreen and take snapshots with the telescopic rather than the microscopic lens.

While taking in the wider picture we shall attempt to learn to listen in stereo as well. If we cannot see what the Bible is depicting without taking in the big canvas, we shall not be able to hear what it is saying unless we tune in on stereo. The two parts of the Bible, the earlier, or Old Covenant, and the later, or New Covenant, are like two speakers in a sophisticated sound system. Only one voice speaks, ultimately it is the Lord's voice, but the sound is projected through twin speakers representing two periods of time. In the first, up until the coming of Jesus Christ, he says *'so much'* but in the following period after the Messiah's coming, he goes on to say *'so much more'*. The latter does not contradict the former but rather the new element consists in the broadening and deepening of the one message. Our hearing is impaired if we persist in listening to only one of the speakers. As we make our journey through the Bible we shall consciously listen in stereo. The earlier and the later revelation harmonize and ultimately we have one message.

To capture the big picture and the full sound of what is happening in the Bible as a whole, we shall visit six locations where God made himself known. Like an address book, the scriptures record the various locations where God chose to be found at different times. At each address we shall meet the same God, but learn different things about him and how he has worked over the ages. On the one hand, there is a great diversity among these addresses and yet, on the other hand, there is a remarkable unity in what we can discover among them all. Each address marks a period in the unfolding disclosure of the divine plan of salvation and is linked to a particular section of the Bible. Over the next few pages we shall find ourselves at half a dozen sites. Hopefully, our appreciation of what is taking place at each location will be enhanced if we take time to look at the relevant Biblical material that sets the scene.

1. In the Garden (Genesis)

2. In the Tent (Exodus, Leviticus, Numbers through to I&II Samuel)

3. In the Temple (I&II Kings, I&II Chronicles, Psalms and most of the prophets)

4. In the Flesh (Matthew, Mark, Luke, John)

5. In the Spirit (Acts and Pauline letters)

6. In the New Jerusalem (Revelation)

At each address the local, the particular and the individual are all very real yet also part of the global, universal and corporate plan of God. All the little people and little things may seem disconnected but in reality they are all part of the grand scheme of God. As in an epic movie, the plot may be analysed frame by frame but every single frame is essential for the final screening. The stills may be enlarged, framed and hung on the wall but it is only when taken together that they make up the dynamic drama. Book by book, chapter by chapter and even verse by verse we may explore God's revelation through the singular history of Israel but we need to keep in mind the much wider context.

What made, and indeed, makes God's people unique is not their analysis of his essence but their experience of his presence (see Exodus 33:16). 'Immanuel', God with us, is one of the major unifying themes of the whole Bible. Knowing his presence is more important than understanding his essence. This has always been, and continues to be, true.

Chapter 1

In the garden

In the beginning

The first letter in the Hebrew Bible is the second letter of the Hebrew alphabet. 'Why?' asked the early rabbis, who scrutinized the text microscopically. These early scholars of the Hebrew Bible had such a fascination with the alphabet that they were tantalized by the fact that God chose the second letter rather than the first to open his written revelation.

Their answer may be dismissed as absurd by the modern interpreter but what it lacks in academic integrity it gains in ingenious insight. As they studied this letter, which incidentally begins the Hebrew word for 'house,' they came up with some striking observations. They observed that this letter has a roof and so no one can go above it. It has a back wall and no one can go behind it. It has a floor and no one can go below it. Their obvious conclusion, as one reads Hebrew from right to left, was that when the reader starts with this letter there is no choice but to go forward. The reader may be fascinated by what has preceded this verse but the text, as given by God, gives us no further information. The Bible is not designed to answer every question about origins that modern minds have. In other words, as readers of the Bible we begin with what God has given and go forward. The Word of God does not begin with proofs of his existence. The text does not tell why or what God is but strikingly 'that' he is. He is there in the beginning but without any indication of his origin.

Like Genesis, only many centuries later, the Gospel of John places the reader firmly 'in the beginning' (John 1:1). As with the original creation, so the 'new creation' in Christ is rooted in the power of the Word. This Word is dynamic and creative. This Word speaks into the darkness and creates light. Furthermore, this Word works in perfect harmony with the Spirit in both settings. In Genesis, it is under the hovering presence of the Spirit that the Word has spoken out creation and it is under the same enveloping presence of the Spirit that the Word is fleshed out in the womb of Mary (Luke 1:35). This Word is spoken in stereo. The first chapter of Genesis reveals 'so much' but the first chapter of John reveals 'so much more' about the Word. It speaks out creation and then lives out incarnation. It is before the world and then in the world. It creates the earth and then lives on the earth. It is 'with God' and then with humanity. This is the Word that was before John the Baptist yet came after him. The God who created in the first place is the same God who recreates. Creation and salvation are the work of the one God. However, if we are ever going to grasp what happened in Galilee we have to begin with what happened in the garden of Eden.

The garden and the city

Paradoxically the most illuminating view of the Garden of Eden may be from the top of the Tower of Babel. That may seem rather strange but I suggest that we climb the tower (Genesis 11) in order to look back over the garden. It is from this vantage point we can appreciate some striking contrasts. At the foot of the tower the city sprawls as an urban challenge to the pristine garden. The enterprise of humanity stands in contrast to the creation by deity. The height of human pride arrogates itself against the wonder of divine perfection. Humanity builds walls behind which many live in shame in contrast to the garden where there had been the opportunity to live in shalom.

To most of us the city is probably more familiar territory than the garden. That's the environment in which we have lived for so long. Humanity is at home on the streets. How can we ever begin to imagine the sheer perfection of that original garden? Untouched by human sin it was flawless. There was neither sight nor sound, touch nor taste to mar the sheer perfection. Even today, after centuries of disintegration, discolouration and disfiguration we still can get glimpses of grandeur. At times we may still find ourselves standing in wonder at some feature of creation. We take in the view, only to slip on a discarded condom, a MacDonald's wrapper or the vestiges of some fast food. In the midst of the splendour there is no escape from the imperfection. Even the most creative imagination will find it impossible to capture that sheer wonder of perfection. It is hard to visualize the garden when we have grown up in the city.

The very first mention of a city in the Bible is strategically placed but often overlooked. Babel cannot be awarded this dubious honour, although it is the place most mental search engines find when asked to locate the first city. In fact the location is alarmingly close to the garden and surprisingly built by one of the first gardener's sons. Just after Cain had murdered his brother he was condemned to be a restless wanderer on the very ground that he tilled originally. God's judgement was too much for him to bear and in this context we read he 'lay with his wife and she became pregnant and gave birth to Enoch. Cain was then building a city and he named it after his son Enoch'(Gen. 4:17). This first city was the prototype for Babel. As Cain recoiled from God's word he determined to secure his own independence, permanency and identity on the face of the earth. While Cain's initial blueprint for the city may not have been on the grand scale of the modern metropolis it was a defiant gesture. If God had been at the centre of the garden, Cain was at the centre of the city. If God had said he was to be a wanderer on the face of the earth Cain was determined to stake his claim in one location. If God had exercised his Lordship by naming the original creation, Cain would usurp that right by now naming his own creation. If the garden was a sanctuary the first city was a hiding place.

Cain could well have been the architect of Babel. The whole atmosphere was permeated by the heady spirit of independence and the quest for permanency. 'Come let us build ourselves a city with a tower that reaches the heavens... *(lest we)*...be scattered over the face of the whole earth' (Gen. 11:4). Moreover they wanted to make a name for themselves (Gen. 11:4). In his stimulating book *The Meaning of the City*, Jacques Ellul, the French thinker, traces a trajectory from this early city through to the modern urban society. Babel is of more than mere archaeological interest to us. The spirit of Cain and Babel lives on in every human enterprise outside the Garden of Eden. If we could only enter some tardis that would take us back into Babel we would be shocked to find that the spirit of the place, if not the scenery, shares much in common with the streets of any modern city. Babel is of interest to us, not simply for an insight into ancient architecture, but for a fascinating exposure of the human enterprise. Whether then or now, the quest for independence, permanency and identity is still to the fore as humanity still rejects God's word as he addresses us in our situation.

Ellul takes us on a spirited ride through time, tracing human rebellion against God in terms of the whole city building enterprise. From Babel it is possible to follow a line through the great building sites of the Bible and to map the human effort to create structures that afforded security and reflected human achievement. Such building programmes were often in defiance of God or at least they were statements of independence from God. The Pharaohs of Egypt are still applauded for their architecture on the grand scale that continues to attract modern tourists. The spirit of Babel was clearly articulated by Nebuchadnezar whose boast about the great city that he had built has been immortalized in the record of Daniel. While the prophets were silent during the period from Malachi to Matthew, one of the great builders in world history was active, Alexander the Great. An architect travelled with Alexander on his conquest of the ancient world and reputedly had plans for a statue of his patron that was so huge that an actual city would be built in the palm of its hand. Water would be collected from the clouds as they gathered around the mammoth head and then channelled down the veins of the arms to supply the city. This was planning on the grand scale. Jerusalem at the time of Jesus had been redeveloped by the grand designs of Herod the Great, who left his mark on the Second Temple of the Jews, and the spirit of Alexander was inherited by the Romans who continued to build to the glory of man. In same spirit Communism used architecture to express power. Hitler, too, employed his own architect, Albrecht Speer, to plan his dream. The spirit of Babel can be found all through history. It was the spirit of Babel that infiltrated the authorities in Jerusalem when Jesus was condemned to die outside the city wall. The city was the antithesis of the garden. As we shall see in the final chapter the city is not beyond redemption, but for most of history as we know it the tale of the city has been, and continues to be, the story of covenant-rejection. Above all, the city is built by human power, exists for human glory and caters to every human whim.

In a typically exaggerated form the rabbis tell a story about Babel that transcends our historical, cultural and geographical distance from it. With characteristic panache they depict the tower as being so high that it would take a person a whole year to climb to the top and equally as long to descend. This was the original statement of 'tower power'. The story goes that when a worker fell from the heights no one bothered, but when a brick fell there was a public outcry. In other words, human life was cheap and replaceable, but they balked at the thought of a whole year's work to replace a brick.

Furthermore a pregnant woman engaged on the building programme barely took time out to give birth before continuing on with the all consuming work. The overstatement is only surpassed by the insight. In the quest for autonomy, humanity has never been more enslaved to work than today. Life has become cheap and the workplace all-demanding. There's always a mountain of work ahead of us. It can be hard to find time for the children. The heights to which we aspire without God only serve to highlight the depths to which we can sink. The tower could only rise from the city. The foundations, ethos and strategy of the tower were alien to the garden for they required a bedrock of human pride.

It is on this trajectory we must also place the twin towers of the World Trade Centre that were devastated by the terrorist strikes of 11 September 2001. At their height these structures represented the height of human achievement and the focus of the faith of many. Where once cathedral spires and church belfries dominated the skyline of medieval Europe, now the high rises of the investment houses and banks indicate where gilt-edge security is to be found. Of course, there can be nothing but forthright condemnation of such a shocking event, and the wave of human sympathy that swept the world was an appropriate gesture of human solidarity. It would be simplistic at best, and totally insensitive at worst, to simply label the horrific attack as an act of judgement. Nonetheless, to the thinking observer, who tries to interpret the world through the lens of Scripture, there are serious issues to be considered. In the space of a few minutes the heights of human achievement were dashed to the ground. The catastrophe was beamed all over the world as it happened and we watched the heights to which man could aspire being wiped out by the depths to which human nature could descend. Before our very eyes the symbols of human success crumbled to dust. Whether in Mesopotamia or Manhattan the warning is the same and the truth remains valid, that unless the Lord builds the house (or, indeed the city) there can be no security against collapse.

The god upstairs

Growing up with the impression that Babel was like an early version of the leaning Tower of Pisa, I found it so illuminating to explore the meaning of the ancient ziggurats that were dotted all over the Mesopotamian valley.

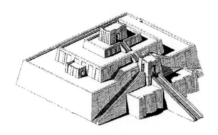

These huge tiered mud brick structures were crowned by temples devoted to the local deities. Like the Babel-builders, the ziggurat engineers were not necessarily atheistic, but rebellious against the true God. Deities were fine provided they stayed up at the top of the structure and did not interfere in everyday life. Surviving records provide fascinating insights into the care of the idols at the top, even to the extent of feeding them daily and providing for their toiletry needs. Occasionally the priests would carry them down and parade them around the city but for most of the time urban life could carry on without them. Sometimes the temple bricks were glazed with blue, creating the impression of heaven from the perspective of the person in the street. They were built to impress, but also to keep God out of everyday living.

It is ironic that the nightmare scenario of the ziggurat may actually provide a fruitful insight into the dream of Jacob recorded later in Genesis. Once again, informed by the Sunday School material of my boyhood, I saw at the centre of this story a extra long extension ladder, readily available at the nearest DIY superstore. I was amazed at the delicate choreography of those angels 'ascending and descending on it' (Gen. 28:12). However, what if it was a ziggurat that had formed the focus of Jacob's dream encounter? The angels were not precariously poised on the narrow rungs but, rather like the priests of the ziggurat, they were going up and down the stairway that linked earth to heaven. At the top of the stairway Jacob did not encounter a dumb idol, but rather the covenant God of his forefather Abraham stood renewing the promise (Gen. 28:13).

While that may be considered dramatic, the story becomes even more riveting when told in stereo. As the redemptive revelation of God unfolds, Jesus will revisit this incident. In the course of his conversation with Nathaniel, the Lord promises the first-century Jew that he will see heaven open and 'the angels of

God ascending and descending', but now they will be 'on the Son of Man' (John 1:51). No man-made stairway could ever reach the heavenly heights, but in Jesus Christ we are offered the new and living way into the very presence of God himself. Rejected by man, God in his mercy and love has actually taken the initiative to open up the way back. In fact, this was the very God who came down the stairway at the first Christmas. He came down into the midst of the very human enterprise that had excluded him. This is a theme we shall return to later as we see his descent into the very heart of humanity and the subsequent reversal of the curse on Babel at Pentecost.

Making a name

As at Babel, so people today want to make a name for themselves. This is a driving force from big business to big brother. This very appetite for a name for one's self is one of the things that pit man in the city against God in the garden. In the biblical record of creation it is God who does the original naming of things that he made. The naming was an aspect of his Lordship. Under him, Adam, made in his Lord's image, was intended to continue to exercise the power divinely gifted to him (Gen. 1:5, 8,10;2:20). However, fallen humanity was not content to name things under God but rather sought to name things after themselves (Gen. 4:17;11:4). Surely one of the most ironic things in the account of Babel is that, despite all efforts to make a name for themselves, not one person is known today. The whole enterprise was a catastrophic failure and the continuing fame game is doomed to the same outcome.

Strikingly in the very next chapter of Genesis God begins all over again with the man of his choice, Abraham. One of the first things that he promises this man of his choice is that he will make his name great (Gen. 12:2). As the opening eleven chapters of Genesis record a widening and ever degenerating spiral from Adam in the garden to humanity in the city, so now there is a new beginning with the focus on the one man. From him, an ever widening series of circles emanate. The city builders wanted to make something for and of themselves but failed. God was going to make something of Abraham. What is quite remarkable is that under the new covenant that same God is still able to make something of us.

The big story begins

The story of our salvation does not begin with our conversion. In a sense it begins with Abraham, and our experience is located on a time-line that starts with him. Our spiritual biography begins with him. That story opens with a God-given promise and what follows in Genesis is not so much a series of disconnected individual biographies as the unfolding drama of a promise. On the one hand Abraham, Isaac, Jacob and Joseph are all unique persons living out particular lives, in real places, in real time. While, on the other hand, the underlying unity is given by the big theme of God's promise progressing through the generations. These men do not merely provide us with a collection of inspiring moral tales but rather allow us to trace God's faithfulness and sovereignty through the strengths and weaknesses of real people, in real places, at real times. In other words, there is a big story or a 'metanarrative' that gives an overarching unity to the particular stories recorded in the Bible. Those first steps of the Abrahamic family from Ur really marked the beginning of what was to become a parade of peoples. Through this one man, Abraham, the nations of the earth would be blessed (Gen. 12:3). The blessings intended for all mankind but forfeited by the city builders would be restored in Abraham. There is a sense in which the journey started by Abraham is still going on and the ever increasing numbers who join his family by faith will be gradually drawn back to a garden where there will be healing for the nations (Rev. 22:2).

For the Christian reading the narrative of the patriarchs, Abraham, Isaac, Jacob and Joseph the experience should be something akin to an Afro-American reading Alex Haley's *Roots*. In that saga, spanning many generations, Alex Haley, a modern Afro-American, traced his family tree back to his forefathers in West Africa. The book had an astounding impact as black America discovered the line that connected them to the continent of Africa. Life in modern America was unintelligible apart from this understanding of the past. In a somewhat parallel way, modern Christians would gain a better understanding of who they are by becoming familiar with the people and events of the more distant past in an equally distant land.

You might be tempted to call this 'history' but let me offer you another way of understanding our place in the big picture. Biblical Hebrew does not have a word for 'history'. History, according to the Chief Rabbi of the United

Hebrew Congregations of the Commonwealth, Dr. Jonathan Sachs, is something that has happened to others but 'memory' is the record of our story. As the Jew looks to Abraham he or she understands this is part of a personal story. Genealogy is crucial to the Jew, and the dealings of God span the generations. That is one of the reasons for the frequency of genealogies in the Bible. Perhaps boring to the modern reader, such lists are so exciting to the Jew who can trace an unbroken chain to the past. However, what is quite remarkable according to the Apostle Paul, writing many centuries after Abraham, is that even Gentile believers may count themselves children of Abraham. Through faith in the work of Christ, the ultimate son and 'seed' of Abraham people like us can be engrafted into this astounding family tree. While writing to the Christians in first century Corinth, Paul refers to 'our forefathers' (1 Cor. 10:1). For years my eye passed over that apparently insignificant monosyllabic 'our' until the full impact struck me. Had you lived in Corinth and were 'in Christ' you had now become part of this drama that had started with Abraham and continued through the wilderness. This was not simply history to you any longer; it had become part of your memory. This was part of your story. Paul was giving the Corinthian believers roots. Brian McLaren captures this so well when he writes of *'The Story that we are in'*. This recently published title reminds me that my experience of saving grace is part of a much greater story. At the heart of this unfolding drama is always God.

With the choice of Abraham we see not only the beginning of an ongoing story but also a penetrating insight into the divine *modus operandi*. Many centuries separate us from our father Abraham but there has been a remarkable consistency in the way that the Lord has chosen to work. Of course, there is diversity in how he operates but the Bible does not make sense unless we appreciate the overarching unity in his way of working. Even though Adam rebelled, he was still the *'man of God's choice'*, introducing a principle that runs through every page of scripture. When Adam failed, God focused again on the one, and with Abraham there begins a series of unique men who would lead to the ultimate man of God's choice, Jesus himself. The blessing that came to Abraham would only come to the nations through him. The great director of the epic of redemptive revelation would keep his cameras focused on the one. The people and events around him may have been real in their own right but always centre stage was the one of his choice. Tracing the line from Abraham, the unfolding promise turns the spotlight on Isaac, Jacob, Joseph, Moses, Joshua, David, Solomon and so on down until the Anointed One himself. Amidst the smorgasbord of religious choices that confront us today, the uniqueness of the Christ is a constant source of offence and yet the divine *modus operandi*, even as far back as ancient Israel, reassures us that God would still have us focus on the man of his choice. The son and seed of Abraham is still at the very core of God's promise.

Before we get to the definitive man of God's choice we shall follow the history of God's promise. In the progressive fulfilment we are going to find God moving out of the sanctuary of the garden in pursuit of a rebellious humanity. Although the story does end with Genesis and it is significant that in the Hebrew Bible the next three books all begin with the little conjunction 'and'. The story links these books together. It is bigger than any individual and any one book. We should not read the Bible with the mentality of the jam-maker. Bible books are not like sealed jars. We need to develop a feel for the themes and concepts that cannot be bottled up in one book, but rather are woven through the scripture as a whole. In search of a profligate humanity, God will leave the garden and move into a tent.

Chapter 2

In the tent

In the cloud

Lieutenant Colonel William Rankin has a rare claim to fame. He is the only man to have fallen through the king of clouds and lived to tell the tale. In 1959, the American pilot was flying at 47,000 feet when he had to eject from his F8U jet over Norfolk, Virginia, due to an engine failure. He parachuted into the middle of a severe thunderstorm that carried him over 65 miles to Rich Square, North Carolina. A descent that would normally have taken about ten minutes lasted forty minutes. During the descent the temperature plummeted to -50 centigrade as he was pounded by hail and buffeted by wind. He was violently sick and on the one occasion when he opened his eyes he found himself looking down a long narrow black tunnel, burrowing through the centre of the cloud. Later he spoke of thunder and lightening that seemed to penetrate his very being. All in all, the interior of a cumulonimbus is not a pleasant place to be! Clouds are awesome. It is no wonder that the Lord hid Moses when he revealed himself in the glory cloud (Exod.33:19-34:5).

Members of *The Cloud Appreciation Society* find blue skies dull. Clouds of any sort, cumulus, cirrus, altocumulus or contrails ignite their passion Sometimes, for those of us who live under the seemingly perpetual grey skies of Ireland, it is hard to share their enthusiasm, but you could certainly argue their case from a study of the cloud in the scriptures. Among the most significant and striking of God's chosen vehicles of self-revelation is the cloud. At once revealing and concealing, the cloud is a fitting choice. Tracing the glory cloud will take us on a trip from Exodus through to Revelation. On the way we can stop off at Jesus' transfiguration and ascension, before experiencing the description of his awesome return to earth 'in the clouds' (Mark 9:7; Acts 1:9; 1Thes.4:17). For the trained eye, the Bible is a cloud-spotter's delight.

WHERE IS GOD TODAY?

Leading the Israelites out of Egypt, God appears in a pillar of cloud by day and a pillar of fire by night (Exod. 13:21). The exodus (literally, the way out) was rooted in the covenantal commitment that the Lord had made to Abraham centuries before. In the final three verses of Exodus 2 there is a strikingly symmetrical little piece of Hebrew word building. No less that four verbs are used to convey the desperation of the Jewish slaves but then four more verbs are used to describe God's response. The Hebrew writers had a genius for balancing ideas; over against the despair of Israel there stands a fourfold answer. The Lord 'heard', 'remembered', 'saw' and 'knew'. At one level, the Hebrew verbs have lost something in translation. A sort of verbal inflation has been at work and these words, like the coins in our pockets, no longer go as far as they used to. For instance, the last verb in the sequence refers to God 'knowing' Israel. This is no mere mental recognition but rather evokes the intimacy, mutuality and reciprocity of the relationship between first man and woman. There, exactly the same verb is used of the man 'knowing' his wife (Gen. 4:1). We shall pick up the loving overtones of this later at Mount Sinai where God takes Israel as his bride.

Furthermore, the fact that God 'remembered' does not mean that he mentally recalled something that he had forgotten. Elsewhere we read of God remembering Noah, Hannah and Samson in distressing situations and in each case the verb indicates his action on behalf of the people (Gen. 8:1; 1 Sam. 1:11, 19; Judg. 16:28). When God remembers he acts and, in response to Israel's heartfelt cries from slavery, he 'remembered his covenant with Abraham' and acted to save them (Exod. 2:24).

Foundational for the exodus event, indeed for the rest of the Bible, was the patriarchal promise. The word of God to Abraham undergirded the action of God on behalf of Israel. At the very centre of this stupendous event we call the Exodus is the key fact that God was bringing this people not simply to Mount Sinai, but to himself (Exod. 19:4). The real high point in the story is not the mountain, but the person of God himself. Nonetheless, as our minds toggle between the earlier and the later events in the unfolding drama of revelation, there is another mountain-top incident that is even more compelling. The temptation to hop from one to the other is irresistible. Crossing the miles and centuries we land on the Mount of Transfiguration where Moses and Elijah converse with Jesus. The English translations of that conversation records that they spoke to

20

Jesus about his imminent 'departure' and, quite naturally, readers will understand this as referring to his visit to Jerusalem (Luke 9:31). On the one hand that is true, but on the other hand there is so much more to this reference. If only the translators had kept the original Greek term that Luke used, none of us would have missed the allusion. The Greek word was *'exodus'*. The geographical reference is there for a purpose but the historical association of the term points us to the ultimate mission of one greater than either Moses or Elijah. Jesus, as the ultimate man of God's choice, was going to complete the definitive act of liberation. What he was about to do outside the city wall was an exodus event. Like Moses, he would confront enslaving powers, bring his people through the experience of death and lead on to the fullness of freedom. This was extreme exodus! The temptation to make the mental jump was too much but we need to return to Sinai lest we get ahead of ourselves. There is an orderly progression in the address book but sometimes the analogies grab our attention and disrupt a neat presentation.

The wedding at Sinai

Sinai is the location for the Mosaic covenant. In the light of the fuller revelation that was to come in the form of the New Covenant, there is a tendency among Christians to undervalue the earlier events. It is true that the later covenant may be superior in many ways, but it would be wrong to deprecate the events on the mountain. No one is anymore aware of the superiority of the new than the Apostle Paul, but even he spoke of the glory of Mount Sinai (2 Cor. 3:7, 9, 10, and 11). That the 'glory' was relative does not mean that it was not real. Yes, it was to be surpassed by a greater 'ministry of the Spirit' (2 Cor. 3:8) but that does not lessen the magnificence of the moment for Israel. Again, if we could only enter our time travel capsule and stand with Moses and the Israelites as they experienced God come down on the mountain, we would surely be awed by the theophany. The glory cloud came down on the mountain and under that hovering presence a marriage was celebrated.

The events at Sinai were set in a new light for me when I discovered that the Jews continue to structure their marriage ceremonies on their forefathers' experience on the mountain. As the Israelites were to cleanse themselves

before the covenant was ratified, so the bride must submit to ritual cleansing in the *mikvah* or ritual bath. The presence of the glory cloud that descended is represented by the *chupah* or canopy under which the ceremony takes place.
As the written tablets provided an objective foundation for the relationship between God and his spouse, so there is a written contract, or ketuvah, drawn up between the newlyweds. This sets Sinai in a much warmer context for me. Admittedly, the Mosaic covenant may now have been surpassed but the God who gave it was no tyrant. He was no Ancient Near Eastern tyrant, but a king who was also a husband and lover. Israel was his bride and he loved her dearly. He wanted to share the greatest intimacy with the one he 'knew' (Exod. 2:25). At the top of the mountain there may have been all sorts of pyrotechnics including smoke, fire, thunder and lightning (Exod. 19:16-19) but equally impressive would be the presence given to the people at the bottom of the mountain. The liberating Lord did reveal himself on the summit, but the loving husband came down to the plain to share a nuptial home, the tent of meeting. This was not to be the last time that God came down to a human level. Without compromising his transcendence, he established his immanence.

Real presence.

The God of glory came down the mountain. He descended to a mobile sanctuary which served as a symbol of his ongoing presence among his people. A principle of identification or solidarity, which will unfold much more fully centuries later, is already evident as the Lord dwells in a tent among a people who are living in tents. The first Christmas is a long way off but clearly the idea of Immanuel was already emerging.

To the discerning eye, the building of the tent is presented in a most interesting way that evokes the creation of the garden. At the very outset the Spirit of God was hovering over the creation scene (Gen. 1:2) and now we find that same Spirit indwelling and empowering Bezalel, a man chosen specifically for the building work of the sanctuary. No mean craftsman, Bezalel was equipped with 'skill, ability and knowledge' by the Lord (Exod. 31:3). This very same trio of terms occur in the Hebrew Bible in Proverbs where they are exactly the qualities attributed to God as he created the cosmos (Prov. 3:19). So the tent builder was not only made, but also worked in the image of his God. English translations of these terms may vary but behind them stands the same three Hebrew words. Whether building the cosmos, the tent or indeed a truly successful life these are vital. The sage personalizes this when he writes that 'by wisdom a house is built and through understanding it is established; through knowledge its rooms are filled with rare and beautiful treasures' (Provs. 24:3). Obviously the 'house' being referred to is symbolic of an individual life or family. Behind the 'wisdom', 'understanding' and 'knowledge' of the New International Version stand exactly the same terms that are translated as 'skill, ability and knowledge' in the Exodus account of Bezalel.

An even more explicit textual reference linking the creation account to the tent building is the Sabbath. After God had instructed Moses and equipped the craftsmen engaged in the tent building, he ordered Moses to remind the people that the Sabbath 'will be a sign between me and the Israelites for ever, for in six days the Lord made the heavens and the earth, and on the seventh day he abstained from work and rested' (Exod. 31:17). On a practical note we may observe that when the rabbis wanted to know what work to rest from on the Sabbath they studied all the activity involved in the tent building and then put a ban on all such things on the seventh day. That rule still stands in rabbinic Judaism.

Like God, Moses looked on all that was done and found that it was good (Gen. 1:31; Exod. 39:43). The tent, like the garden, was a sanctuary where God was with his people and he had a lot to teach them.

Teaching is actually one of the key purposes of the five books of Torah. Few words have suffered greater injustice at the hands of translators than the Hebrew name of the first five books of the Bible. Usually rendered by 'law', the term now conjures up ideas of an oppressive God who sits like a big policeman waiting to catch people out. What a difference it makes to discover the family tree of the word Torah. Like most Hebrew words the great, great, great grandparent is a three letter verb which was used to convey the idea of shooting an arrow. Obviously, the archer deliberately points the arrow in the desired direction. Over the centuries that idea of guidance or direction leads naturally into the realm of instruction or teaching. So, rather than conjuring up the vision of a policeman waiting with his speed gun to catch the unsuspecting motorist, this word is meant to take us into the realm of loving instruction and guidance. To borrow a name from a Jewish website, the Israelites were the original 'Torah Tots'.

God's kindergarten.

Kindergarten, or children's garden, is understood worldwide as the initial stage of a child's education. When Friedrich Fröbel, a young German academic, started the first such school in the 1830s his intention was to emphasize the importance of activity in learning. One of his most original ideas was the use of the so-called Froebel gifts, a set of geometric wooden blocks. By means of these he sought to make the child aware of the environment and, in the process, built up a bond with the adult who was guiding the play.

Centuries before Froebel, another master pedagogue was at work in the Sinai wilderness. The Lord, who had liberated his people from slavery set about forming them into a very special group. In a sense, the Tent of Meeting was the scene of the prototypical kindergarten. Having redeemed his child, Israel, from the oppression of Egypt, he was now going to shape this people in a very special way. The setting of the tent provided an ideal classroom where every sense was going to be employed in the learning. Design and building of the structure is recorded in Exodus but the initial curriculum is outlined in Leviticus. Sadly this is a book that has been seriously undervalued by modern Christians. A sort of pre-school of redemption, this material must be read using every sense that God has blessed us with. The splendour of the high priestly garments catches the eye. The nose is excited by the aroma of spices and the smell of burning flesh. There is wax on the hands as they come in contact with the heads of sacrificial goats and bulls. Sounding shofars (rams' horns) demand the attention of ears. Moreover, there is feasting to be enjoyed in the course of many of the ceremonies. In this early classroom in the wilderness a master teacher bombarded his pupils with sights, sounds and smells.

If the method of teaching was innovative and effective, the substance of the learning was to have lasting value. Things learned at this preliminary stage were of no value if they had to be repudiated in later life. Truths learned in kindergarten may be elementary but they are accurate. Perhaps the child who played with coloured blocks may go on to become a professor of mathematics but the fundamental fact that two plus two makes four remains true. A fact may be learned in pre-school in a most elementary way but time does not diminish its accuracy. Whether a pre-schooler or a post-graduate, the person uses the same fact but with different levels of comprehension. Perhaps the analogy may be imperfect, but to a degree the New Covenant is rather like post-graduate school. Richer and fuller things are revealed but they do not contradict foundational facts laid down at an earlier stage. The history of salvation is given progressively and the later parts may expand, but do not contradict, the earlier chapters. The 'new' of New Covenant does not imply that nothing existed before first page of Matthew but rather what follows is so much fuller, richer and deeper than what has gone before.

It can be very profitable for us to return to this wilderness address where God was introducing some of the most basic facts about salvation. All the concepts and the very vocabulary that has become so familiar in Christian circles were hammered out on the anvil of early Israel. Here we shall meet terms like sacrifice, blood, sanctuary, priest and redemption. Even an exploratory visit to this classroom should convince us that we could increase our word power substantially just by exploring the vocabulary. Thousands of pages have been written about this material but we shall simply highlight some of the big ideas.

Sin is serious.

To the novice the Book of Leviticus may seem like a nightmare. Sometimes known rather disparagingly as 'the butcher's bible', the middle book of the Torah seems quite out of place in modern society. Incidentally, the very fact that it stands in the middle of the five books could be quite telling. Hebrew thought often put key ideas in the middle rather than at the end of a piece of writing. That Leviticus is third in a series of five may be an indication that the content, and not just the position, is pivotal.

The initial temptation, or possibly frustration, on reading this material is to get bogged down in the mass of detail. Almost instantly the reader is surrounded by dismembered animals, blood, oil, grain, flour and unfamiliar aromas. If that is the case then the unsuspecting soul needs to be guided to a vantage point in order to take in the wider context. While the detail has its place, there is surely an overarching theme which is the gravity of sin. Sin is serious and it must be dealt with. It is so serious that only God can deal with it. Over the span of seven whole chapters God spells out how in his holiness he cannot tolerate sin, but in his grace he provides the means of grace for the people to approach him. It is he who will deal with the sin that separates and it is he who opens up a way back into his presence.

One very helpful suggestion from some commentators is that the term 'sacrifice' which is so prevalent in this section is actually misleading to many modern minds. That term implies giving up something of a value to self for the sake of another or a greater good. Often the emphasis is placed on the cost to the giver. For instance, in chess a forward-thinking player may make a positional sacrifice, losing something with the intention of winning even more. Parents may sacrifice for the sake of the children's education. The problem arises when this type of thinking subtly insinuates itself into our relationship with a holy God. The 'sacrifices' outlined in these chapters have been misunderstood as the price humans pay to win God's favoured response. As in the gym, so here, the mentality seems to be that if there is no pain there will be no gain! This is absurd. Already the story of Exodus makes plain that God has intervened to save on the basis of his gracious initiative. His favour is not bought by human sacrifice but sinful humans do need a divinely appointed means of grace whereby they may respond to this loving and liberating God. In this light, the word 'sacrifice' could be meaningfully replaced by 'offering'. In fact, this idea better conveys the original term in the text. Once again, a little genealogical research on the term 'offering' will reveal that it has family ties with the idea of drawing near or approaching. Even in Modern Hebrew it has a close link with a term meaning 'relative' or someone who is close to you. What a different light this then casts on these chapters. Fundamentally they are actually about a God-appointed means of how a sinful humanity can draw near to the holy God.

Access is possible.

If sinful rebellion took humanity 'East of Eden' then one of the primary object lessons to be learned at the tent is that God provides a way back into his presence. Expelled from the eastern gateway of the garden, mankind was barred from re-entry by two sword-bearing cherubim. The depravity of the human condition in exile is illustrated, not only by the Biblical account of the flood and Babel, but more recently in John Steinbeck's famous novel *East of Eden*. This best seller, first published in 1952, retold the story of Cain and Abel as it traces two families, the Hamiltons and the Trasks, over three generations. For them, and for the rest of humanity, Eden proves totally elusive. However, there is grace in the Biblical story and the tent in the wilderness is about God taking the initiative to actually create a way back into his presence. Detailed instructions about the orientation of the tabernacle take on a new significance when it becomes clear that the gateway to the courtyard and the door to the tent are always on the east. The openings on the east were sending out a clear signal that God was making access possible. In this new structure the sword-bearing cherubim who barred the gateway were now replaced by two other cherubim who marked the divine presence in the inner sanctuary (Exod. 25:10-22).

If access was now possible it was also controlled. The clear message was that there was a way to God but that it was a way of God. A large part of the kindergarten curriculum focused on the person and role of the priest. As the priests in general and the Great High Priest in particular take centre stage, we return to a theme that we met in Genesis, the man of God's choice. Crowned with a golden plate attached to his turban, the high priest was designated as 'holy to the Lord' (Exod. 28:36). At the same time he wore the names of the twelve tribes engraved on precious stones on his chest and shoulders (Exod. 28:11, 15-21). A model of perfect manhood he stood representing both God and humanity. He was the divinely appointed mediator standing between the Lord and his people. One with the Lord and yet one with the people, he stood as the ultimate go-between. Through his office the Israelites could draw near to God. Yet again as we listen and watch the whole epic of redemption we can see why the much later writer of Hebrews cast Jesus in the role of the ultimate High Priest, through whom 'a new and living way' was opened into the presence of God (Hebs. 10:20).

The way back to God for a sinful humanity was mapped out in an elementary way in the kindergarten. There, the lessons were taught clearly. Sin was so serious that only God could deal with it satisfactorily and in doing so he created a way back through the mediator of his choice. There was still another major area to be covered in the syllabus and that was holy living.

Holiness is practical.

Such is the ad hoc nature of the topics covered in the last section of Leviticus (chps.17-27) that it is difficult to subsume them under one heading. However, if we were to choose one term then it would have to be 'holiness'. Abraham Heschel, the Jewish philosopher, once described 'holiness' as the most precious word in religion since it uniquely describes the very nature of God himself. This God who has no equal, and is beyond comparison, revealed himself, not only to Israel, but also through Israel. The very lives of the chosen people were to reflect the nature of this holy one. Even a cursory reading of these concluding chapters of the manual of holy living makes it clear that the covenant life included the use of time, sexual ethics and even food consumption. Holiness is not intended to be abstract. Holiness is practical. Holiness has more in common with a workman's tool chest than a delicate figurine on the mantelpiece. It is to be expressed in action rather than admired from a distance. These people were to be the very embodiment of God's nature. They were a particular people chosen to convey a message that would ultimately go universal.

God was not simply at the heart of the camp but he was at the very heart of everyday life. Towards the end of Exodus it is the unfaithfulness of the people that jeopardizes that presence. When the people turned their worship to the golden calf the covenant God threatened to withdraw his presence (Exod. 33:3). Paradoxically, it is the context of this dilemma that we have one of most stupendous revelations of the Lord. In response to the pleading of Moses, the Lord comes down the mountain in the cloud to proclaim his name. He passed in front of Moses proclaiming, 'The Lord, the Lord, the compassionate and gracious God, slow to anger, abounding in love and faithfulness, maintaining love to thousands, and forgiving wickedness, rebellion and sin. Yet he does not leave the guilty unpunished; he punishes the children and their children for the sins of the fathers to the third and fourth generation' (Exod. 34:5-8). Martin Luther referred to this verse as the sermon on the name and in Jewish circles it is known as the Thirteen Attributes. When I read these verses I always think on one of those huge North American freight trains. At the head there are usually two great power horses hauling an endless chain of loaded wagons snaking behind. At the rear comes the guard's van. As the Lord reveals himself, he declares his name twice, such is its power. It is as if once is just not enough. Wagon after wagon follows and each one overflows with some distinct aspect of his nature. Not even a lifetime would allow enough time to unpack one fully. Compassion, grace, mercy, love and patience roll out and yet the guard's van is there at the end to make it clear that none of these are at the cost of his justice. This is the nature of the Presence that would be with Moses and the people in the tent (Exod. 33:14). At this address we meet the Liberator and Holy One in whose presence there is rest.

Chapter 3

In the temple

Shattered glass

The sound of shattering glass marks the final element in a Jewish wedding. The groom deliberately smashes the glass by stamping on it. A note of great solemnity is introduced to the festivity. Traditionally this jarring moment in the midst of all the joy is interpreted as a reminder of the destruction of the first two Jewish Temples. So deeply engrained in the Jewish psyche is the idea of the temple that even at the moments of greatest joy the anguish is remembered.

The history of the Temples is a long and complex one but for our purposes we shall employ three images to help us interpret the significance. There are lots of places where you may go to explore the architecture and events surrounding the building but our purpose is to see its role in a much bigger drama. The temple may be seen as a milestone, marking progress in the unfolding revelation of God; a foundation stone, focusing attention on a specific place of God's choice; and a touchstone, providing a standard by which Israel was measured by the prophets.

Milestone – measuring time

While Christians measure history before and after Christ, Jews date everything in terms of Temple Periods. As God's plan sweeps through time, the temples stand rather like milestones, pointing both backwards and forwards.

Most modern motorists speed past old mileposts but these historic stones marked the way for ancient travellers and helped them measure distance. Enthusiasts, dedicated to the preservation of the milestone, tell us that it was the Romans who first placed these markers along their roads. Everything radiated from the Golden Milestone standing at the heart of Imperial Rome. Distance was measured in order to aid the timing of troop movement and every thousandth double step was marked by a large cylindrical stone. It is easy to see how this stone became known as a milestone when we appreciate that the Latin word for one thousand was *'mille'*. In one sense these stones were like an early Global Plotting System, helping soldiers locate themselves in relation to their home city.

I find it helpful to think of God's progressive revelation of himself and his plan of redemption as a roadway that runs through time. We begin in Genesis and journey toward the climactic events of Revelation. It is enormously exciting to think that even today our own Christian experience places us squarely on that road that started with Abraham. On the one hand, we have something to journey towards as we anticipate the climax of God's plan but, on the other hand, it is good to take time to look in the rear view mirror to see what is behind us. A glance in the mirror reminds us where we have come from. We are part of a much bigger story that keeps unfolding. Just as the warning on the wing mirror says that objects are much nearer than they appear, so a look into Bible helps us appreciate these events in the past are not as distant as they may appear at times. They are an essential part of the one big story that we are also taking part in.

As we journey through history there are major mileposts such as the Exodus, the conquest of the land, the monarchy, the exile and the coming of the Messiah. Each one of these has its own significance but it is also only part of a much bigger scheme of things. Some of these events cover decades, or even centuries, but no matter how long they are, we find that they are still part of something much grander. No matter how fascinating any one of these periods might be we cannot linger there interminably. History is going somewhere. God's plan is unfolding and we dare not stay too long in the one place or in the one time. Though the temple spans centuries, the plan of God covers millennia. Like other stages in this sweeping drama, the temple periods may be studied but also need to be set in context. The God who had come to dwell in the Temple was the one who had been in the tent and also in the garden.

Whether in the tent or the temple the Lord was nonetheless declaring an amazing solidarity and identification with the people and place of his choice. In the desert, where the people had lived in tents, the Lord was also in a tent but as they settle in the land of Canaan and build houses of stone we find the Lord dwelling among them in a building of stone.

The First Temple Period stretches from the time of David and his son Solomon (around 1,000 BC) until Jerusalem fell to the invading Babylonians in 586BC. There followed a period of exile during which many Jews were deported to Babylon and those left in Jerusalem lived without a temple. The rise of Cyrus the Great of Persia spelt the demise of the Babylonian Empire and his new policy of multiculturalism allowed Jews to return and rebuild their temple in Jerusalem. This rebuilding marked the beginning of the Second Temple period. It was this same temple that would be remodelled by Herod the Great many years later and dominated the skyline of the Jerusalem that Jesus visited. So prominent was this sanctuary on the landscape that it was known as the nose of the world. According to some, it was seen as the most striking feature on the face of the earth. It was also described as the neck of the world, the vital link between heaven above and earth below. Even more graphically it was portrayed as the navel of the universe, the centre of everything else. To this day, Jews mourn its destruction at the hands of the Romans in year 70AD. So these two so-called Temple Periods sweep us through a major part of Biblical history. Beginning with King David's plan to build the sanctuary the temple story takes us down to Jesus, the Son of David's prediction that not one stone of this building would be left standing (Mark 13:1-2). In the comfort of our armchairs it is easy to forget that Bible history races through centuries. As we turn pages we journey through time and for centuries the Jerusalem Temple stands as a significant milestone. It is hardly an exaggeration to say that to trace the history of the Temple is also to trace the history of the Jewish people. In that sense it functions as a milestone marking a stage in the unfolding drama of redemption. It could not be understood apart from the past. The very layout and all the priestly service were derived from the tent. It pointed to the future in as much as the rule of God on earth was localized in the city and king of God's choice.

Foundation stone – focusing attention

To borrow an analogy from the world of physics we could say that there is a powerful centripetal force at work in the course of Israel's history. Recourse to a little bit of Latin, as well as Physics, will help us here. Centripetal is a double-barrelled word deriving from the Latin *centrum* ("centre") and *petere* ("tend towards"). So a centripetal force is one directed towards a centre or axis. It draws to a central point. In some senses the Jewish temple functioned like such a central point for many centuries of Israel's history. It was the focus of attention and was designed to be so in certain respects by God for a period. That is not to say it was to take attention away from him but for a time it was an important instrument of his revelation. From the outset it was intended to be an instrument rather than merely a monument. Of course, as we shall see later, the means to an end has always the potential to become an end in itself. Developing this picture of the centripetal force, we could say that there were actually two centres to which the Lord wanted to draw attention. Firstly there was the king, who was the man of God's choice, and secondly there was the temple, the place of God's choice. The two are inseparable. Just as at an earlier period the role of the priest was unintelligible apart from the tent of meeting, so now at this later stage both the throne, on which sat the king as the man of God's choice, and the temple, in which the presence of God was located, were both located in Jerusalem. In the flurry of all the activity spanning a millennium between the rise of King David and the birth of Jesus, the Son of David, we can take our bearings from these two foci. There are just so many incidents and fascinating lives during this period that could absorb our attention and lose us in the detail. Of course, God is in the detail but our purpose is to keep the big picture in view. The particulars should not blind us to the universal plan. Throne and temple may function as binoculars, simultaneously giving us a key to viewing God's intentions in history.

Like the first temple, the first king of Israel is introduced in somewhat ambivalent terms. Against the clamorous backdrop of the days of the Judges, Israel cried out for a king. That in itself was not necessarily a bad thing but the cry was poisoned by the fact that they did not just want a king; they wanted one like all the other nations around them. Israel's uniqueness as a witness to God was jeopardized and so the prophet Samuel objected to this initial call. The prophet realized that his nation's demand for a king was tantamount to a rejection of their true king, the Lord, who had liberated them from Egyptian bondage. Samuel was deeply displeased 'so he prayed to the Lord. And the Lord told him: "Listen to all that the people are saying to you; it is not you that they have rejected, but they have rejected me as their king."…Now listen to them; but warn them solemnly and let them know what the king who will reign over them will do." (I Sam. 8:6-9). So God gave the

Israelites what they wanted but their first experience of kingship under Saul was anything but positive. Against the backdrop of Saul's catastrophe, something very significant was to develop. Having virtually decommissioned Saul whom he had appointed in the first place, Samuel was commissioned to anoint David as the next king of Israel.

As the shepherd boy is chosen as Saul's successor, it is as if the great director of this epic story of redemption turns the halogen spotlights fully on the star. David takes centre stage and assumes a place in the unfolding drama, far more significant than his mere humanity would merit. Like Abraham and Moses before him, he is the man of God's choice and for a period he would give us something of an insight into what it meant to embody the rule of God in a man on the earth. He was neither more nor less a human being than any of us but for that period he was chosen for a divine purpose. The choice of a particular person at a specific period is a key feature of God's modus operandi. Throughout the stages of progressive revelation there are certain consistent elements in the divine strategy. Although the whole plan spans centuries, even millennia, these recurring tactics would seem to indicate that God has known the plan of campaign from the outset. From our vantage point in time we can look back to see that through the changing times of Abraham, Isaac, Jacob, Joseph, Moses, Joshua, David and Jesus there was the continuing focus on the one of God's choice. History moves on, cultures change but the focal point of redemptive revelation is the one of God's choice.

If the focus on the one man is sharp, so too is the innate human resistance to the one who is chosen for God's specific purpose. Psalm 2 opens a fascinating window on this human reaction to God's anointed. Read these verses and let's transport ourselves back into the armchair of an ancient near easterner watching the evening news bulletin. The lead story of the day is the coronation in Israel. Both national and international broadcasts are dominated by the event. All the leading channels have sent their reporters to record the day's happenings. The crowning of a king in Israel drew world attention. What is striking is that the broadcast is not so much concerned with the actual pomp and pageantry of the day, but rather the international reaction to the new king. In fact the editorial team decided in advance to give no detail about the ceremony, but to go immediately to the international reaction. As the cameras take us on a tour of neighbouring capitals, a series of correspondents report on the overwhelmingly negative reaction to this new king in Jerusalem. No sooner has he been enthroned than international coalitions and conspiracies are launched against him. Aggression and bitterness characterize the responses from the government spokesmen and women of the world powers of the day. Why was there such intensity in their feeling?

To plumb the depths of this antipathy we must appreciate something of the meaning of monarchy in Israel. Despite the cry of the nation for a king like the other nations, the Lord had given Israel a king whose role was actually distinctive. On the one hand, the king of Israel was a man but, at the same time, his office had deeper significance. In fact the man chosen to rule in Jerusalem was to embody the rule of the living God on earth. Of course, not every king lived up to this ideal but the shortcomings of human rulers do not take away from the divine ideal. The king in Israel stood apart from, and in opposition to, all other earthly rulers. As the 'Anointed One' in Jerusalem, the monarch was to be an expression of God's rule on earth. God's active sovereignty was personalized in the man of his choice, the king, and localized in the place of his choice, the temple. However, human nature has always seemed to prefer pluralism over against such narrow exclusivism. Whether in the ancient or the modern world people have been more comfortable with systems of thought that recognize more than one ultimate principle or person. No less than the modern multicultural society's offence at the teaching that salvation is found in Christ (*Christos* is a Greek word meaning *'anointed one'*), ancient pluralistic culture resisted the idea that God's rule was embodied in the one of his choice. This innate human hostility is vividly portrayed in the opening verses of Psalm 2. '...the nations conspire...and the peoples plot...the kings of the earth take their stand and the rulers gather together against the Lord and against his Anointed One'(Ps. 2:1-2). The coronation stirred up opposition from all around. The rulers of the nations did not take kindly to the ruler of the world being represented in Jerusalem.

What makes this newscast so unusual is that we have reports not only from the leading cities but we have an exclusive comment from heaven itself. Half way through the story the scene shifts from the newsroom on earth to the throne room in heaven. Having heard the policy makers express their hostility, now we hear from the Lord of glory. The earthly tirades are met by heavenly laughter. 'The One enthroned in heaven laughs, the Lord scoffs at them' (Ps. 2:4). The Lord of history is neither surprised nor intimidated by their opposition. The one on the throne of Israel, the 'Anointed One', may be rejected by people on earth but he has been placed there by the power in heaven. All on earth will have to reckon with him. Ultimately they will live in subjection to, or rejection of, the one whom God has chosen. Even at this very early stage, about a millennium before the coming of the Messiah ('Anointed One'), we see something of the divine modus operandi. We dare not rush ahead in history but the principles of new covenant revelation are beginning to emerge. The king of ancient Israel, as the chosen of the Lord, drew hatred to his person and office just as Jesus, the ultimate embodiment of God's rule in the flesh, would do in the centuries that were to come.

If the news is grim, the forecast is actually good. Despite the rejection of God's 'Anointed One' by the rulers of the earth, the future hope of the nations of the earth actually rests in him. God's purposes cannot be thwarted and his kingdom will eventually be universal.

No mention is ever made of the actual king who is the focus of this coronation psalm. It may have been the coronation of David or some other monarch but the essential point of the poem remains the same, irrespective of the person. Neither human powers nor plotting are able to undermine the plans of God in the one of his choice. While many kings punctuate history, David must take his place as one of the most significant figures in the line of God's choice. As the shepherd-king, David was the first in a line of succession through which we can trace the purposes of God. A fascinating play on words allows us to see David not only as the builder of the house of God but also the founder of a house that served God. God is the master builder and there is more to his house than stones. This play on the word for 'house' links the man on the throne to the God in the temple.

Once secure on the throne, King David proposed that he would build the Lord a permanent house. Up until this time the tent had functioned as the mobile sanctuary but David had the idea of a stationary dwelling place. In response to this idea the Lord promised that not only would David build a house (sanctuary) for him but that he would build a house (family) for the king. 'The Lord declares…that the Lord himself will establish a house for you: When your days are over and you rest with your fathers, I will raise up your offspring to succeed you' (2 Sam.7:11-16). Both in Hebrew and English we can play on the word 'house' to indicate either a home or a household. David's son Solomon was to build the temple in stone but the Lord would 'build' the household in flesh and blood. The record of the former is recorded in the early parts of Kings (1 Kgs.3-11) but the story of the latter spans much of Kings, Chronicles and brings us down to the birth of Jesus himself. The story of God's 'building' the house of David is the history of the Israelite monarchy. Tracing this story, we race through the centuries following a line of both good and bad kings. The story can be complex in places. It is not as simple as good kings versus bad kings. Sometimes the good and the bad compete intensely in the one person. For instance, Solomon was a paragon of wisdom and yet a polygamist and idolater. He built the temple that his father dreamed of and yet introduced untold pagan shrines that his wives worshipped at. This complex tension of positive and negative attributes may be found in many, if not all, of all the kings of David's line. Where the good is evident we have a foretaste of the perfection of the ultimate Son of David, and where we see the bad we are compelled to see how much we need the perfect Son of David. Each one of the kings lived and ruled as an individual in his own right and yet each one had his place in the plot of a much greater narrative that would climax in Jesus himself.

Of striking interest is that the record of these kings and earthly kingdom of Israel is told in a section of the Hebrew Bible known as 'The Former Prophets'. The Book of Kings reads like history to our Western minds but paradoxically it is classified as prophecy in the Bible that Jesus would have known. Those Scriptures that Jesus would have used while teaching on the Emmaus Road were divided into Torah (instruction), Nevi'im (prophets) and Ketuvim (writings). Luke alludes to this threefold division in his account of the post-resurrection activity of Jesus (Luke 24:44). The second division or 'The Prophets' began with Joshua, Judges, Samuel and Kings. Our modern minds may struggle to understand these as prophets. Isaiah, Jeremiah and Ezekiel spring to mind as prophets, but not Joshua or the storyteller of Kings. However, to the Hebrew mind prophecy was not just about predicting events in the future. It was primarily about interpreting the events of the present by the standards God had instituted. Prophets in ancient Israel have actually been referred to as exegetes of existence by one leading Jewish thinker. These individuals were uniquely equipped to interpret the politics of human behaviour through divine lens. They measured the kings by God-given criteria but we shall return to this in the next section of this chapter.

The history of the household or line of David is inseparable from the story of the house or temple of the living God. Even a brief survey of the kings of David highlights the fluctuating faith of the people. With kings like Josiah we reach the heights of godliness but with other like Manasseh we descend to the depths of depravity. To trace the monarchy is to take a roller coaster ride that is both thrilling and sickening at one and the same time. Yet all the while 'the Lord is in his holy temple' declared both the psalmist and the prophet. (Ps. 11:4; Hab. 2:20). The earthly sanctuary stood to remind Israel of the reality of the heavenly throne. In the dizzying whirl of history the temple stood immoveable at the vortex. Geographically and theologically the temple stood at the centre of this period and at the heart of this building is the room where the Glory of Lord came to dwell.

Throughout the great song book of the Temple, the Psalter, we hear of the great joy and honour of going up to the House of the Lord. Perhaps the so-called Songs of Ascent derived their name from this very activity, although some suggest this name from the ascent of the steps within the actual temple courts. As pilgrims walked up the long and arduous wadis (valleys) to Jerusalem they would encourage one another by singing about the goal of their pilgrimage, God's house on the hilltop. Their songs would focus the mind's eye on the sanctuary where they would celebrate the major festivals. While the Jewish year was punctuated by the *mo'edim*, or God's appointed times, there were three in particular that required the participants to actually make the journey to Jerusalem. These three were Passover *(Pesach)*, Weeks *(Shavuot)* and Tabernacles *(Succoth)*. According to Deuteronomy (16:16 and see also Exod. 23:14-17), Jerusalem was to be the focus of these pilgrim festivals. In some small measure it is still possible to recapture something of what the atmosphere must have been like by visiting the Jewish Quarter in the Old City of Jerusalem on a Friday evening. As the sun sets and Sabbath approaches people pour onto the streets. The crowds are pumped through the maze of arteries in the old city towards the heart of modern Judaism, the Kotel, or Western Wall. These stones, which are all that remain of Herod the Great's Temple Mount, exercise an irresistible pull on the prayerful who gather there. It is possible to pay a virtual visit to the wall, thanks to modern computers and web cameras, but only an actual visit allows you to savour the atmosphere. Down through the centuries the Temple Mount had this powerful centripetal force on the Jewish people.

From our vantage point in retrospect it is easy to see how the 'milestone' could become a monument. The signpost became for some a shrine. By the time of Jeremiah (late 7th and early 6th centuries BC) superstition had crept in. 'The temple of the Lord, the temple of the Lord, the temple of the Lord,' (Jer. 7:4) became a popular mantra. The prophet was called to challenge the vain and repetitious babblings of the crowd. Similarly, Ezekiel dramatically exposed idolatry even within the sacred precincts of the temple when he 'went in and looked, and ...saw portrayed all over the walls all kinds of crawling things and detestable animals and all the idols of the house of Israel' (Ezek. 8:10). Despite the early warning sounded by Solomon in his dedicatory prayer that the Lord could not be contained in this mere building (1 Kgs.8:27), the place became virtually deified in popular credulity. So deeply engrained was the adoration of architecture that only the destruction of the building and a period of exile in Babylon would break the stranglehold.

However, it was not just among the ancient Jews that people were tantalized by the stones. Very early on in my first pastorate in a small lumbering and mining community in North America I had an interesting encounter that focused on Solomon's temple. It was a good natured exchange with an elderly gentleman on a bright afternoon in his conservatory. With my mind's eye I have a vivid picture of him sitting opposite me with his Bible in one hand and a book about Freemasonry in the other. He was totally convinced that my theological education was insufficient when it came to understanding the temple of Solomon. There were mysteries and esoteric truths that I, as a mere Christian reader of the Bible, could never access. He claimed, as indeed did his neighbour just down the road, that there were secrets in the early sanctuary that I could not be privy to while uninitiated. That conversation has never left me. It presented me with a challenge to search out if the real message of the temple was to be found in the historic stones or the ultimate living Stone upon whom the kingdom would be founded. Is the mystery of the building to be perpetuated or was it revealed in the coming of the Son? We shall return to this in the next chapter but in the meantime that conversation serves to remind me that in the story of divine revelation milestones point us forward while monuments lock us in time. How many modern congregations have become myopic because they cannot see beyond the building where they meet? Buildings, whether they be churches, cathedrals or temples may have their place in the plan but ultimately they were never intended to be any more permanent than the Tent of Meeting. God is going somewhere in history and no matter how grand the architecture, it is at best for a time and only for that time. Ironically, the very building which became the object of Israel's superstition and other's fascination was the touchstone used in divine judgment.

Touchstone – judging standards.

At the heart of the Book of Deuteronomy, which is the great manifesto for life in the promised land, the Lord had appointed one central place of worship. To Israel he said, 'you are to seek the place the Lord your God will choose from among all your tribes to put his Name there for his dwelling. To that place you must go (Deut. 12:5). Defying the countless shrines and high places of a myriad of Canaanite deities, the unique God of Israel put his Name, or his presence, in the one place of his choice. This location became not only the definitive place of worship but also the measure of national religion. This is particularly clear as we read the history recorded in the Book of Kings. Later, the writer of Chronicles focus our attention again on the temple but from another perspective. To appreciate the different angles that both books take on the temple it is crucial that we make ourselves familiar with an outline of Jewish history from the conquest of the land onwards. A simple timeline will give us the basics.

Joshua Conquest	Dark days of Judges	United monarchy Saul-David-Solomon	Northern Kingdom		Exile	Return under Persian power
			Southern Kingdom Line of David			

The foundation of Israel's history was laid in the promises given to Abraham. The history of those promises brought us out of Mesopotamia, into and then out of Canaan, down to and then up from Egypt before leaving us in the wilderness on the east bank of the Jordan. As Deuteronomy ends, Israel is poised on the river bank for re-entry to the Promised Land. The story continues in Joshua which records the conquest. Had this been a fairy tale then probably the Israelites would have taken the land and lived there happily ever after, but this is the Bible. This is the record of God's dealing with real people and rather than a happy ending the reader is taken into the dark days of the Judges. These were days of infidelity and immorality. Indeed, by the end of the Book of Judges, it seems as if immorality gives way to total amorality. It is during this period that the popular cry goes up for a king like all the nations and, despite Samuel's protestation, he anoints Saul as the first monarch in Israel. Saul and his successors, David and his son Solomon, rule a nation united in name at least. Even in the days of Solomon the seeds of schism begin to spout and on his death the kingdom splits. The northern tribes follow Jeroboam while the much smaller southern kingdom submits to the rule of Solomon's son Rehoboam. Up north a series of kings manage to hold onto power until the kingdom succumbs to the merciless might of Assyria around 722BC. The line of David keeps its grasp on the southern throne until about 586 when the state and the temple fall to the invasion of the Babylonians. Years of exile followed until the new power of Persia emerged. Under the aegis of Cyrus the Great, reknowned for being ahead of the times with his policy of multiculturalism, the exiles were allowed to return and rebuild the temple.

In order to try to understand this period and the Bible books that record it we are going to choose two vantage points to view events. Firstly, in our minds we are going to travel back to about 586 BC. Jerusalem has fallen and the first temple has been rased to the ground. There are obvious questions in the mind of every Jew who observed the trauma of these events. Why was God allowing this to happen to his chosen people? Had God not promised his presence permanently in the place of his choice? After centuries of Torah observance what had they done to deserve this judgement?

Joining us in our viewing platform is the compiler of the books we know as Kings. He has some interesting answers to these questions. Through his eyes we go back to the last days of King David and review the events leading up to the start of the exile.

As he takes us back through the history of Israel he measures the nation by four criteria that are found collectively only in the final book of the Torah.

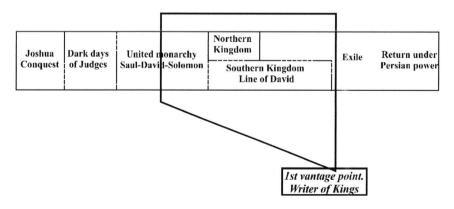

From Deuteronomy he applies the same standards that some of the prophets would use in weighing up the people. Firstly, he illustrates how the Israelites had consistently refused to heed the warnings of the prophets despite the fact that the Lord had said that he would put his word in the mouths of his spokesmen (Deut. 18). Secondly, their kings, both northern and southern, had consistently fallen short of the divine ideal (Deut. 17:14-20). Thirdly, and of great interest to us, worship had been decentralized. Despite the one place of worship appointed in the Torah (Deut. 12), new centres had been built at Dan and Bethel in the north while innumerable high places had been erected even in the south in the vicinity of Jerusalem itself. So, fourthly, when judgment came it was simply God doing what he said he would do. He had warned that he would scatter a disobedient people among the nations (Deut.28:64) and this is precisely what happened in the exile. Our historian friend who compiled Kings is actually called 'the Deuteronomist' in some academic circles because he compels us to read history through the lens of the fifth book of the Torah. Viewing history from his perspective can be quite depressing but we do get the rationale behind the flattened temple and the dispersed people.

Now we move on to our second vantage point and this time we are joined by another historian. Cyrus the Great of Persia is on the throne. Assyria and

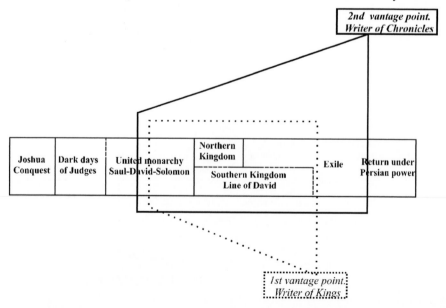

42

Babylon are powers only in the past. Persia is now the super power of the age and under the new policy of tolerance the Jews are allowed to return home. While the writer of Kings had given the reasons for the razing of the temple, our second historian, the Chronicler, will provide us with hope in the raising of the temple.

Even a cursory glance at the diagram is informative. Immediately we see that Chronicles spans more or less the same period as Kings but what makes the difference is the radically different perspective. We shall see shortly that the Chronicler does actually cover a longer period but there is a reason for that. It is nonetheless true and hopefully it will prove helpful to us as readers to see that we are revisiting the same period, but reviewing it from a totally different lens. The post-exilic vantage point sets things in a very different light. The Chronicler makes for a brighter companion in many ways as he proposes to give hope to those returning home. Once again we shall find the temple figures prominently in his thinking.

No longer is the question 'what did we do to deserve this punishment?' but rather 'do you think that God is still interested in us as a people after the exile?' 'Yes, most emphatically, yes' says the Chronicler and central to his response is the attention he gives to the rebuilding of the temple itself. For him all arrangements and administration relating to the sanctuary are significant but above all the location of the foundation stone is important. This may be illustrated in a rather subtle way. When the earlier Deuteronomic historian recounts the life of David he gives us a no-holes-barred assessment. Despite being the man of God's choice, the former shepherd is party to adultery, illegitimacy and even murder. Of course all of these human shortcomings contribute to the failure of the kingdom and provide the ammunition the writer needs to explain the judgement when it came. However, the David of Chronicles seems a very different character. Not one of these major failures is even mentioned but in an apparently random way the Chronicler selects only one sin of David, and even that seems relatively insignificant to us as modern readers. The sin that comes up for particular mention is the numbering of his fighting men (1 Chr. 21). Perhaps to us that seems rather innocuous in comparison to his greater misdeeds. Nonetheless for a man whose road to kingship had started by felling a giant warrior with a pebble slung in God's name, it was not a good sign when he started to boast in the size of his army. That David knew he was wrong in measuring his military might was evident in his response to the prophet who rebuked him and accordingly he set about demonstrating the sincerity of his repentance. Under the economy of the Old Covenant David could only atone for his error by making an offering. To do that he required an altar. To build an altar he needed a piece of land. To acquire the land he negotiated with the owner, a man called Araunah, the Jebusite. All very interesting, you may observe, but are such details vital to the unfolding history of the redemption of the world?

Only when we remember that the Chronicler was trying to encourage the returnees who were about to rebuild the temple in Jerusalem can we make sense of his version of David's life. As they planned for the future temple it was imperative that they knew where the first temple had stood. By retelling the story of David's sin the Chronicler intended to point out the original site which had been on the threshing floor of Araunah the Jebusite that had been purchased for the king's altar. Knowing with accuracy the first site was so important for the new builders and how better to point it out than by telling this story of David's acquisition of it.

While the temple is a key feature of the Chronicles and David is a key person, the book does not actually begin with him as we might imagine. Certainly God's covenant with David was a bedrock for assurance for those coming back home but the Chronicle wants to point out that God's interest in them as a chosen people did not begin with the shepherd boy who became king. That is why the very first person in the Book of Chronicles is no other than Adam! To those who were worried that God had forgotten them during the years of exile the message is sounded loud and clear. The Lord's love for his people started as far back as Adam and continued right up until their time. That unbroken commitment is then traced through nine solid chapters of genealogy. Reading these chapters is sheer boredom to so many modern readers but to the original readers it was the history of unending love that spanned generations and gave every individual name a place in history. In some ways the Chronicler was like an early Alex Haley, pointing the people to their 'Roots' and bringing them up to date.

While Chronicles is tucked away in the heart of what we call the Old Testament, it is actually the very last book in the Hebrew Bible. Therefore the reader of the Hebrew Bible ends with his or her eyes being directed by the Lord, the God of heaven, to rebuilding of the temple in Jerusalem. The Hebrew scriptures end with the summons to go up to Jerusalem. As Cyrus decreed, 'The Lord, the God of heaven, has given me all the kingdoms of the earth and he has appointed me to build a temple for him at Jerusalem in Judah. Anyone of his people among you – may the Lord his God be with him, and let him go up' (2 Chr. 36:23). So off we go…but there are surprises in store!

Chapter 4

In the flesh

Body talk

If God does not have a sense of humour, he certainly knows how to be ironic. The first Christmas illustrates this vividly.

Jesus was born into a world that had been shaped by the legacy of classical Greece. That age had set a standard in art and architecture not merely for the ancient world but for much of the western world today. In museums and glossy holiday brochures temple columns symbolize much of the glory that was Greece. What is seldom realized is that these great architectural masterpieces were influenced by the human body. Bodies and buildings were linked in the minds of antiquity. The proportions of the human body were taken as the measure and standard of beauty of all things.

One of the most famous illustrations of this is the so-called Vitruvian Man, made famous in the drawings of Leonardo Da Vinci. Better known as the man in the square and the circle, the Vitruvian man is so named because he was first drawn by a Greek temple architect called Vitruvius. This ancient mastermind wrote a lot about building and was fascinated by the study of symmetry and proportion in the design of temples. For him the proportions of the human body were fundamental in achieving beauty in any structure and so he dictated that the proportions of the building should follow the proportions of the body. His studies had shown him that the circle and the square were the perfect figures from which to generate building designs. Probably all of us have seen what is surely his most famous drawing of a spread-eagled human figure in the centre of a circle and a square. His calculations had shown him that the distance from the tips of the two outstretched hands was the same as that from the top of the head to the tip of the toes. The belly button was right in the middle of both the square and the circle. Now, if you are given to experiment, there is something that you may want to test out sometime.

If you have decided to read on rather than spread-eagle yourself on the floor, then you will surely agree that there is a certain irony in the fact that pagan temples were inspired by the human body which Vitruvius and others thought was made in the divine image. Houses of stones, reflecting the symmetry of the human body, were constructed to accommodate the pagan deities of the Greek world. These buildings are still being admired by the modern tourist. However, at a crucial moment in history, the Creator God, who had for a period chosen to live in a stone edifice, now chose to live in a human body. That first Christmas marked the point when God rejected the temple of stone in favour of a temple of flesh. Is there not more than a hint of irony in that action? The Glory of God was no longer to be found in a building but in a body. The miracle of the incarnation marked another great milestone along the road we are travelling.

Along this roadway we have stopped off in the garden, the tent and the temple. At each place the Lord's presence indicated his identity with his people. Hopefully by now we are getting a sense that the road is going somewhere but that the destination is known only to God. Sometimes the road is more clearly defined and identifiable than at other times. There are times when we sense that there is more than one lane. Perhaps, if we were to use the analogy of ocean currents rather than lanes it may be more helpful. Within the Bible we sense that there are some very strong currents carrying the reader forward. Some are obvious but there are others that are at work on a deeper level. With the help of the New Testament writers we are going to try to identify four of these major currents that sweep us through the Hebrew Scriptures and converge in Christ. The force of the movement will carry us

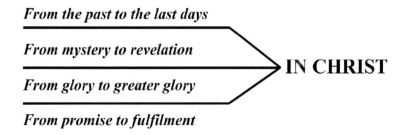

From the past to the last days

From mystery to revelation

IN CHRIST

From glory to greater glory

From promise to fulfilment

forward even allowing us to jump over the blank page between Malachi and Matthew. As we are carried along we should not ignore the detail of history but the prevailing current will keep us focused on God's bigger plan. The tidal flow carries the Bible reader from the past into the last days, from mystery to revelation, from glory to even greater glory and from promise to fulfilment. Dominating these last days, revealing the mystery, reflecting the glory and fulfilling the promise is the figure of Jesus Christ.

From the past to the last days (Heb. 1:1-3)

With one inspired stroke of his pen, the writer of the Letter to the Hebrews divides world history into two major blocks.. He asserts that 'in the past God spoke to our forefathers through the prophets at many times and in various ways, but in these last days he has spoken to us by his Son.' His opening lines are unforgettable. For him all that exists are 'the past' and 'the last days'. Not for him the interminable debates that divide historians about when periods of history begin and end. What matters is that a major defining event has occurred in the history of the world, that has produced the irreversible division between what was 'the past' and what is now 'the last days'. Not only would the coming of God's Son 'cause the falling and rising of many in Israel' (Luke 3:34), but also he would mark the ending of one age and the beginning of a new age.

It is as if the writer grabs his reader, lifts him or her out of the living room armchair and straps them into the cockpit of the space shuttle. After a lifetime of looking out the living room window, the cosmic view from the pilot's seat is now astounding. The familiar local scenes framed by the window are now replaced by the strangely new universal vista. This is a totally new perspective. So often in Bible reading, concentration is focused on one small passage framed for us by the daily notes but there are times when we need to look through the shuttle window rather than the magnifying glass. There is no one better at creating such a grand view than the writer of Hebrews. From his perspective all of God's revelation activity in the world falls into two periods, 'the past' and 'the last days'.

In terms of God's revelation of himself 'the past' may be described as piecemeal, partial and preliminary. Content-wise it was fragmentary and incomplete. Time-wise it was periodic and unpredictable. Nowhere under the earlier covenants did God disclose himself fully. At best 'our forefathers' got glimpses. At most they gleaned insights. In relative terms they had very little when measured against what was to come.

Jesus Christ, Son of God coming into the world, was God speaking to humanity as he had never spoken before. This revelation marked the climax of history. Content-wise it was clear and definitive. Time-wise it was final and lasting. 'Now he has appeared once for all at the end of the ages' (Heb. 9:26). In his Son, God not only introduced 'the last days' but he effectively spoke his last word to this world. There is no indication that this message was to be supplemented or amended by any later prophets or cult figures. In actual fact, through Christ he is offering the world its last opportunity and so the writer adds his solemn injunction, 'today, if you hear his voice, do not harden your hearts' (Heb. 3:7). Though writing to first century Christian believers, he sees a clear analogy between their position and the intransigence of the generation of Israelites who had left Egypt and died in the wilderness. One group was as stubborn and as vulnerable as the other. Threats to the spiritual life were as real in the world of the first century as in the wilderness.

One of the fascinating features of this writer's pen is the ease with which it can toggle between the early history of Israel and the early days of the church. For him the coming of Christ may have sliced world history in two but it did not threaten the fulfilment of God's promises. Rather, from the vantage point of the shuttle window, the reader now sees the wonderful sweep of the master plan. In stark contrast to those who want to ignore or deprecate what they call the Old Testament, we see that the first century writer draws extensively upon the earlier writings. Instead of opposing the old and the new, it is as if he says in the earlier revelation God has said 'so much', but now in Christ he is saying 'so much more'.

This puts pay to the notion that the God of the Old Testament is some vengeful deity full of wrath who stands in stark contrast to the New Testament Jesus who comes meek and mild. If you reread the opening verses of Hebrews and pay close attention to the verbs it becomes apparent that there is only one God who speaks. 'In the past **God spoke** to our forefathers through the prophets at many times and in various ways, but in these last days **he has spoken** to us by his Son'(Heb. 1:1-2 emphasis mine). The God who 'spoke' in the past is the very same God who 'has spoken to us by his Son'. The tense of the verb changes, but not the subject. It is the one God who speaks through the ages.

Not only does God speak with one voice but he is engaged in building only one house. In the third chapter God's activity in history is likened to that of a master builder. While looking at his promises to David we got a glimpse of this 'house-building' not simply in terms of the temple but also the household of the king. Buildings are secondary in this divine activity. Above all God is creating a people for himself and in Israel he started to lay the foundations. As this house started to rise, Moses played a crucial role as a faithful servant, but at a much later date Jesus Christ was to be recognized as 'son'. While Moses had been a servant in the house, Christ is the son who is head over this house. The contrast between the two men is striking but so, too, is the continuity of the one house. Moses and Christ were both part of the one programme. One may have been the servant and the other the son, but both are active in the same house. There is only one house being built, one voice speaking and ultimately one God in the Scriptures. In Christ, the one mediator between God and man, these truths come into sharp focus.

With all our stress on the unity and continuity in the unrolling programme of revelation and redemption, we need to be careful not to ignore the disparate elements and the discontinuity. A Bible reader has to use both hands. On the one hand there are those rich unifying themes that run through the whole book and yet on the other hand there are things that make the New Testament really new. However, that it is 'new' does not mean that everything after the first page of Matthew is created out of nothing. What makes it new is the unprecedented breadth, depth, and clarity with which the revelation now comes. What had been partially revealed in a piecemeal and preliminary way is now given with a fullness hitherto unknown. The Book of Hebrews is a wonderfully clear example of this.

This book is best read through a triangular lens. The three corners represent the elements of correspondence, contrast and superiority. Each one of these help us appreciate what is going on in the New Covenant. For example we meet the figure of the high priest in Hebrews. His person and office **correspond** exactly with his forerunner in the days of the tent and the temple. However, when Christ is described as the great High Priest there is not only the link with the past but there is a strong **contrast**. Like the previous priests he is a mediator but in contrast to the others his service is perfect and eternal. In this latter aspect lies the **superiority** of the office he exercises in the new order of things. Similarly, when we read of the heavenly sanctuary in which Christ now serves we naturally make the connection with the earlier sanctuaries of tent and temple but see the contrasting superiority that makes the later one overshadow the earlier ones. In 'the past' we are introduced to the concepts, offices and vocabulary of redemptive revelation that are then revealed so much more clearly in 'the last days' with the coming of Christ. As the current sweeps us through from 'the past' to 'the last days' we move from the preliminary to the final revelation. What begins as partial gradually moves towards fullness. Mystery becomes revelation in Christ.

From mystery to revelation (1 Pet. 1:10-12)

If we find some of these ideas hard to get our minds around, then perhaps it will be of some comfort to realize that we are not the first. I love the totally disarming honesty of Peter who makes some great confessions in his letters. Firstly, he admits that he finds some of Paul's writings 'hard to understand' (2 Pet. 3:16). Surely many of us can identify with him on that point. The Bible may be accessible to us all but that does not mean that it is all easily understood. Secondly, he takes us by surprise by insisting that as far as the plan of salvation is concerned we as New Covenant believers can grasp more than any angel or prophet who has gone before us. In fact he insists 'the prophets, who spoke of the grace that was to come to you, searched intently and with the greatest care, trying to find out the time and circumstances to which the Spirit of Christ in them was pointing when he predicted the sufferings of Christ and the glories that would follow. It was revealed to them that they were not serving themselves but you, when they spoke of the things that have now been told you by those who have preached the gospel to you by the Holy Spirit sent from heaven. Even angels long to look into these things' (1 Pet. 1:10-12).

Take another moment to reread these verses that Peter wrote. However, now every time you meet the word 'you' mentally replace it with 'us'. Now we find that 'the prophets, who spoke of the grace that was to come to *us*, searched intently and with the greatest care, trying to find out the time and circumstances to which the Spirit of Christ in them was pointing when he predicted the sufferings of Christ and the glories that would follow. It was revealed to them that they were not serving themselves but *us*, when they spoke of the things that have now been told *us* by those who have preached the gospel to *us* by the Holy Spirit sent from heaven. Even angels long to look into these things.'

Do you feel drawn into the text and into the scheme of things? We live on the same side of the death and resurrection of Jesus as the recipients of Peter's letter. We live out our lives, like them, in the times between the Lord's first and second comings. That places us in the same position in terms of the unfolding plan as first-century saints. What had been a puzzle to prophets and angels has now become plain to them and us who have embraced the truth of the gospel. We are no longer just interested bystanders or occasional observers but active participants in this great unfolding story. In 'the past' (Heb. 1:1) the prophets had been given truth but only so much. What a privilege to find that we have been given 'so much more'. The same Spirit who was at work in the prophets' lives now works in ours, but he did not reveal the fullness to them at their point in time.

To put it another way, they had to live with mystery but we live with revelation. Of the twenty seven appearances of the word 'mystery' in the New Testament, twenty one of them are in the letters of Paul. Witness the excitement of the apostle as he announces that 'the mystery that has been kept hidden for ages and generations…is now disclosed to the saints' (Col. 1:26). He knew that now ordinary believers in Ephesus could understand things angels had not been able to grasp. When reading the letter addressed to them, the Ephesians would gain an 'insight into the mystery of Christ, which was not made known to men in other generations…(but)…has now been revealed by Spirit to God's holy apostles and prophets' (Eph. 3:5). With the coming of Christ an age had dawned when the mystery would be revealed, but not just to Colossians, Ephesians or Romans, but to the world. On this great universal note Paul ends his letter to Rome, giving glory 'to him who is able to establish you by my gospel and the proclamation of Jesus Christ, according to the revelation of the mystery hidden for long ages past, but now revealed and made known through the prophetic writings by the command of the eternal God, so that all nations might believe and obey him – to the only wise God by glory for ever through Jesus Christ! Amen' (Rom. 16:27).

Let's disabuse ourselves of any notion that Paul's concept of mystery was the same as Agatha Christie's or, for that matter, the so called mystery cults of his own day. Cults, guilds and associations abounded in the Greco-Roman cities of the first century. To live in the Greco-Roman world was to live in a spiritual supermarket. Life was not compartmentalized into political, religious, social, and economic realms. Rather religion was embedded in all everyday activities. There were associations and guilds for all types of trades, including fishermen, clothing and leather workers, stonemasons, potters, physicians, bakers and entertainers. Such groupings catered to popular religious appetites, created business opportunities and defined social identity. Members would gather regularly for a meal, enjoy some entertainment and make an offering to their patron deity. Often the religious element of their society revolved around closely guarded secrets which none but the initiated would ever know. Obviously the very nature of these groups means that little was written down but the ancient cult of Cabirus affords a fascinating glimpse into one. Cabirus was murdered by his two brothers. Racked with guilt, the brothers mounted the victim's head on a spear, wrapped it in royal purple cloth and carried it to Mt. Olympus where it was dedicated and then buried. The stuff of legend became the 'mystery' at the heart of the cult. Members were initiated in special robes, confessed their sins and submitted to a water baptism and a symbolic immersion in the blood of their hero. Gatherings often degenerated into drunken sexual orgies but always the 'mystery' was at the centre. The spiritual universe of the Greco-Roman world was thickly populated with such deities and percolated with mysteries. In many respects the form may have changed but not the appeal to the modern person. Esoterica, deep secrets and mysteries still exercise a powerful gravitational pull on our Godless but hungry society. That Dan Brown's novel 'The DaVinci Code' became virtually a cult phenomenon witnesses to this fact.

In answer to both the ancient and the modern quest the Apostle Paul provides the key to the real mystery that is found uniquely in the Lord Jesus Christ. This mystery is the last word in God's plan which had been formed even before the creation of the world. From the outset God had intended that it would be realized in the fullness of time and in the fullness of his revelation in his son. Unlike his contemporaries, Paul understood the mystery, not as an attainment, but as a truth prepared and revealed by God alone in Christ. We could say this was God's best kept secret and all along he intended to share it, but not a moment before his appointed time. What preceded the disclosure had its own glory but was nothing in comparison to what would follow. The glory housed temporarily in a tent and a temple was really best suited to a human body where the fullness could dwell.

From glory to greater glory (2 Cor. 3:7-18)

Gradually it is becoming clearer that down through the ages and pages of the Hebrew Scriptures the truth was only revealed in a partial way. Partial does not mean that it was imperfect. Preliminary does not mean that it is now to be discarded. Sadly there are both Muggles and Marcionites in the church pews. The former, fictional creatures who populate the world of Harry Potter simply do not take the spiritual world seriously while the latter, historical beings, who take their name from a second century heretic, do not take the Scriptures seriously. Marcion taught that the God of the Old Testament was not the true God and rejected the Hebrew Scriptures entirely. If we liken the two testaments to the speakers in a stereo system then Marcion would insist that we listen only in mono. As a result many in the church have been impoverished and have never heard the rich fullness of God's addressing us. To insist upon the necessity of the Hebrew Scriptures is at worst offensive to some and at best superfluous to others. Nonetheless, a powerful challenge comes from the Apostle Paul himself. Forcefully Paul writes to the early believers in Corinth that the old covenant may have been temporary but it was also glorious in its own time. He takes the Corinthians back to the events at Mount Sinai. He affirms that 'if the ministry that brought death, which was engraved in letters on stone, *came with glory*, so that the Israelites could not look steadily at the face of Moses because of its glory, fading though it was, will not the ministry of the Spirit be even more glorious? If *the ministry that condemns men is glorious*, how much more glorious is the ministry that brings righteousness! For *what was glorious* has no glory now in comparison to the surpassing glory. And if *what was fading away came with glory*, how much greater is the glory of that which lasts! (2 Cor. 3:7-11 emphasis mine). From the normal perspective of New Testament believers we tend to see the sheer superiority of what came with Christ. Yet does Paul give us the mandate to deprecate all that went before and rob it of the glory (limited but no less real) that marked it? Surely not!

Sinai may appear quite early in God's address book but when the Glory-cloud came down on that mountain something quite stupendous took place. At the end of our second chapter, while exploring the tent, we explored how God revealed his name to Moses from the mountain. His Glory-presence came down onto the mountain in the form of the cloud and he 'proclaimed his name' (Exod. 34:5). While the Lord was revealing himself to Moses the revelation was nonetheless only partial. In fact the Lord told his servant that at most he could only see his back but his face 'must not be seen' (Exod. 33:23). From a Hebraic point of view his name is virtually equivalent to his true nature. His name is not a mantra given to initiates but a declaration of who he is. Sometimes before an ancient battle, warriors would write the name of their enemy on a piece of pottery, dance themselves into a frenzy and then smash it violently on the ground. Having destroyed their opponent's name, they believed they had broken his power and so would go out to defeat him on the battlefield. Against this type of background we can begin to appreciate why the Lord said that his people were never to take his name upon their lips for nothing. Literally that is what he commanded them in the Decalogue (Exod. 20:7). The name and the nature of God are synonymous. Possessing his name did not mean that the people should think that they could manipulate their deity. So even when the Lord reveals his name to Moses there is still so much of him wrapped in mystery. Moses gets to see so much, but God's 'face must not be seen' (Exod. 33:23). At best Moses' view is veiled but the exciting thing is that a day would come when God would show his face so much more fully and the veils would be no more. While Moses saw God's back, the Apostle John would see his face in its glory. It is a huge leap from a prince in Egypt to the prologue of John but the text helps us dramatically.

Jewish commentators speak of the thirteen attributes of God being revealed to Moses on the mount. For our purposes two of these are highly significant. The Lord describes himself as 'abounding in love and faithfulness' (Exod. 34:6). In Hebrew this reads *'rav chesed va-'met'*. These are terms that are weighed down with rich significance. *'Chesed'* is that powerful determined love and loyalty unique to God and *''met'* is truth which is of his very essence. Keeping this astounding insight into God's nature in mind let's leap forward to the first century world of John's Gospel.

The prologue of the Fourth Gospel is one of those truly astounding pieces of literature but the writer's intention was to impress us with the glory of his God rather than his prose. That Word that had spoken creation into existence had now become flesh in Christ. In him 'we have seen his glory, the glory of the One and Only, who came from the Father'(John 1:14). To see Jesus is to see God in other words. Then John concludes with an arresting phrase. He declares that 'the One and Only' is 'full of grace and truth'(John 1:14). Perhaps the heart-stopping excitement is best appreciated when we turn from English back to a Hebrew edition of the New Covenant to discover this phrase is '*chesed va-'met*' – the very same phrase that described the God of the Exodus. English translations do vary and so it is not so easy to see this parallel phraseology in them but it is inescapable if we read the scriptures in Hebrew. Perhaps you are thinking that the New Testament is written in Greek. Yes, that it is true but the men who wrote it were Jews and so thought like Jews. While writing in the widely accepted language of the Greco-Roman world, their material can very easily, and often meaningfully, be back translated into Hebrew. Such effort is more than amply rewarded when we discovered jewels like the recurrence of the phrase '*chesed va-'met*'. While Moses could only see 'the back' of his God, John could declare that God was showing us his face in Jesus. There is even more to discover when we explore the contexts of both Moses' and John's encounters with God.

In broad terms both the passages in Exodus and John share the idea of God dwelling with his people. The former depicts this in terms of the Tent of Meeting while the latter sees fuller realization of the concept in the Word dwelling among us in Christ.

Apparently John deliberately intends to evoke the earlier portrayal of God's dwelling in the tent. When he tells us that 'the Word became flesh and made his dwelling among us'(John 1:14a) he makes a tantalising choice of verb. What he opts for is a verb related to the noun, '*skene*', which means dwelling. In turn this word 'skene' is thought to be related to the Hebrew word '*shekinah*' which means glory but is derived from a verb that meant to settle, inhabit or dwell. The significance of the fact that the Hebrew word for the Tent, '*miskhan*' is actually derived from the same word should not be lost on us either. If we can negotiate through this maze of words and their meanings, then something very striking emerges. A complex of ideas gel to communicate something simple yet profound. In effect, John is saying to us that in Jesus Christ, God, who literally pitched his presence among the Israelites at the foot of Sinai, is now in our neighbourhood and is showing us the glory of his face. Where Moses had had a veil we have been granted a full exposure. Where there had been a tent, now there was a body. Where there had been glory now

there was even greater glory. Where Moses could only have a partial glimpse
of the glory, Simeon could cradle the glory in his arms.

From promise to fulfilment (Luke 2:29-32)

Old Simeon, the saint who had spent so much of his life waiting for the
promised Messiah, cradled the ultimate paradox when he opened his arms to
the child Jesus. He was so excited that he was ready to die! With a passion
he turned to God. 'Sovereign Lord, as you have promised, you *now* dismiss
your servant in peace (Luke 2:29 emphasis mine). The veteran of many years
of anticipation encapsulated a world of meaning in that one little
monosyllable, '*now*'. His prayer or poem of praise lives on in many traditions
as the '*Nunc Dimittis*', a name derived from the Latin Vulgate which begins
'*Nunc dimittis servum tuum, Domine*'. From this comes the beautiful
rendering of the 'Book of Common Prayer', 'Lord, now lettest thou thy
servant depart in peace'. At one and the same time the small three-letter word
marks both consummation and inauguration.

In terms of the former, centuries, if not millennia, are condensed into that one
word. Simeon's '*now*' marks the climax of a long wait. The older I grow the
more I am impressed by the amount of waiting there is in the Hebrew
scriptures. The years between Genesis and Malachi prove a salutary corrective
to instant-mania of so much modern Christianity. There days, weeks, months,
years and even centuries are spent biding God's time. God had made promises
to the patriarchs but the road to fulfilment must often have seemed like a long
dark tunnel. Just imagine what it must have been like for Godly men and
women living under the reign of Queen Athaliah, a daughter of Ahab and
Jezebel who ended up on the throne of David in Jerusalem. Talk about irony!
Like her mother in the northern kingdom, Athaliah determined to wipe out the
prophets and terminate the line of David. Her reign of terror lasted for about
seven years and to the ordinary people she seemed to achieve all she set out
to. Only the tiniest handful of people actually knew that one young prince of
David's line had been secreted away beyond the wicked queen's grasp. For the
rest it must have seemed like the rule of the Ice Queen over Narnia – always
winter but never Christmas! There just seemed to be no hope at all. There
was only one thing to do and that was to wait and hold onto the promises God
had given. Waiting has never been easy but it has been widespread. Abraham,

Jacob, Joseph, Moses, Job, the Psalmist and Simeon all spent a lot of their lives waiting. Even today many saints must live with a wait on their minds. God seldom seems to send in fast response teams but he asks his people to trust and bide his time.

Simeon's exclamatory 'now' must be understood against this backdrop of the ages. When he uttered it he was punctuating time. The long wait was over. His outburst was an exclamation of surprise and a full stop marking the end of an age. Perhaps the best commentator on Simeon's outburst is the Apostle Paul. In passages that we have already referred to in another context, Paul points to 'the mystery of Christ, which was not made known to men in other generations as it has *now* been revealed by the Spirit to God's holy apostles and prophets' (Eph. 3:5 emphasis mine). What had 'been kept hidden for ages and generations…is *now* disclosed to the saints' (Col. 1:26 emphasis mine). To put it yet another way, for Paul 'the time had fully come' (Gal. 4:4) and God's plan reached a consummation point in the coming of Jesus. Appropriately, Simeon's response is a piece of Hebrew praise, a veritable little mosaic masterpiece of allusions to the earlier covenant. Within the space of a few lines he sweeps from promise to fulfilment and from the national to the universal. Now he holds Jesus in his arms. Now he has seen God's salvation. Strikingly the word 'salvation' is a play on the name of Jesus himself! 'Jesus' came down to us via Latin and Greek but originated as the Hebrew 'Joshua', or more fully 'Yehoshuah' which means 'Yahweh is salvation'.

However, the point of consummation is also a point of inauguration. So much had been revealed and fulfilled but there was so much more to come. Now the 'day of salvation' had begun (2 Cor. 6:2). In academic circles this little word 'now' has attracted an phenomenal amount of attention. Truly, its value is inversely proportional to its size. It is one small word with a huge meaning. If you like technical jargon, you will appreciate that some scholars have labelled this word 'the eschatological now'. Eschatology is widely recognized as the study of the last days and that is exactly what the 'now' indicates, the dawning of the last days. We have already looked at the opening verses of Hebrews where the coming of the Son marked the watershed between 'the past' and 'the last days' and we can expand this even more. Simeon obviously knew his Hebrew scriptures and he recognized that, as the waiting was over, so something radical and universal was beginning. With Jesus there began a time of unprecedented revelation and salvation. As Paul exclaimed, '*now* is the time of God's favour, *now* is the day of salvation' (2 Cor. 6:2 emphasis mine). Even if he was writing in Greek, he was thinking in Hebrew. The twin phrases reflect the Hebraic pattern of parallelism as he affirms that 'the time of God's favour' is the same as 'the day of salvation'. The reference is to the period of time between the comings of Christ. We are living in that '*now*'.

Both Simeon and Paul were excited by the dawning of a new age. The 'now' is inseparable from the 'new'. For them the 'age to come' that Jews had been longing for had burst into history. As Jews, Simeon, Paul, and indeed Jesus, would have divided time into 'this age' and 'the age to come'. Dividing those two periods would be the definitive moment when the Messiah came. There are Jews who are still waiting for their Messiah, but for Simeon and Paul the birth of Jesus was the coming of the Messiah. In other words, for them, 'the age to come' had been inaugurated. With Jesus 'the past' was gone and 'the age to come' had been launched. This is precisely why Paul was so exuberant when he exclaimed that 'if anyone is in Christ, he is a new creation; the old has gone, the new has come!' (2 Cor. 5:17).

From a different perspective Jesus makes the same point in a significant conversation with the woman whom he met at a well near Mount Gerizim. Between the two of them one of the most important dialogues in the history of redemption took place and John devotes over half of the fourth chapter of his gospel to it. In the course of the interaction between these two very different people something quite astounding was affirmed by Jesus. I doubt if ever any demagogue has made a more radical claim but here in the course of what must have seemed like a normal exchange Jesus made a statement that challenged and changed centuries of religious practice. Central to what he said is our little word 'now'. He asserts that the centuries old temple-worship of both Samaritans and Jews was about to be replaced since 'a time is coming and has *now* come when the true worshippers will worship the Father in spirit and truth, for they are the kind of worshippers the Father seeks' (John 4:23 emphasis mine). In one sentence he launches a devastating blow against centuries of Jewish and Samaritan tradition. Everyone knows about the Jewish temple in Jerusalem but few realize that archaeologists have uncovered the foundations of one equally as big on Mount Gerizim, the focus of Samaritan worship. Jesus's bold claim was a shock to Jew and Samaritan alike. It was not that he was abolishing worship but rather he was re-rooting it. True worship would no longer be literally in any building but rather in *spirit* and *in truth*. Surely we are justified in adding *'in Jesus'*. Sitting with the woman at that well Jesus decentralized worship. No longer was it localized in any earthly temple but it was now universalized. It was no longer tied to a Near Eastern piece of real estate. People could engage in true worship anywhere in the world. Being *in the spirit, in the truth* and *in the name of Jesus* was more significant than being *in* a temple, church, cathedral or meeting house in Jerusalem, Rome, Canterbury or Geneva. That Samaritan woman took home much more than the bucket of water that she had come for. Leaving home for a drink she was returning with a revolutionary announcement that would change the world. She had met the Messiah and effectively witnessed the demolition of the most sacred buildings of her day. The temples in Jerusalem and Gerizim may have been still standing physically but she knew that all that they ever represented was now embodied in the man with whom she had been talking. God had met her in Jesus.

This is precisely the point that Matthew, a former tax official, was making when he wrote his account of Jesus. At the outset of his story he describes Jesus as 'Immanuel' which he then interprets for his reader as 'God with us' (Matt. 1:23). Then at the very end of the same gospel he tells us that the last words on the lips of Jesus evoked this name as he said 'surely I am *with you always*, to the very end of the age' (Matt. 28:20 emphasis mine). It is as if Matthew is telling us that between these two verses, at the beginning and end of my account, lies the story of Jesus who was God with us as never before. The God who had been in the garden, tent and temple had come to express an unprecedented identity with his people. This was the ultimate in plane truth! He had come to walk on our level. Truth was made plain on our plane.

Yet nothing is ever quite what it seems. How could Jesus, who was about to leave the earth, make a promise that his presence would be permanent among his people? How could he be with them 'always' and yet go to be with his Father? Apparently if he was going to be absent in the body he was planning to be present in another way.

Chapter 5

In the Spirit

Standing where Jesus did not jump.

One of the most interesting places in the world is a place where nothing actually happened. To this day anyone may go there. Simply the best thing to do is to stand still and contemplate what did not happen there. The precise location is a spot in the ancient city of Jerusalem.

A maze of arteries pump people through the Jewish Quarter to the heart of the Jewish world, the Western Wall, or the Kotel as it is called. Standing there in prayer, a visitor cannot help but sense the heartbeat of the Jewish people. If you have never been in person, I am sure that you have seen a postcard or even paid a virtual visit via a web camera. After a moment to absorb the scene, I would invite you to turn right and walk southwards along the bottom of the western wall of the Temple Mount. A few metres will bring you to the sharply defined corner where the Western Wall ends and the southern boundary wall begins. This is the place where I want you to stop. Just stand still for a moment. Look around and look up. As you look around you will see the evidence pointing to this having been a very busy corner. Looking back up the Herodian pavement that follows the Western Wall you will see the remains of a row of shops that would have been packed with pilgrims before the destruction of the Temple by the Romans in AD 70. As you look up you need to remember that the original height of that corner would have been at least double what it is today. There is neither sign nor shrine to suggest this place has any significance. There is nothing to mark a momentous event in the past. However, you may well be standing at the very spot where Jesus did not jump! That is precisely the non-event that makes this exact location so significant.

Some years ago a large stone was found here. On that piece of masonry was a Hebrew inscription, 'the place of trumpets'. Apparently this had

WHERE IS GOD TODAY?

fallen from what had been the highest point at the south-western corner of the Herodian temple mount. From the niche carved in this stone the priest would sound the shofar to mark the Sabbath and major festivals. Tradition even had it that from that very spot the trumpet would sound to announce Messiah's coming. This may well have been the very corner where the devil took Jesus when he tempted him to jump. Had he employed a modern spin doctor among his disciples, then probably he would have been advised to jump and catch the headlines. However, Jesus knew that the heavenly kingdom could not be established in an earthly way. Rather than jumping from a wall, he knew that he would have to be nailed to a tree. So, on the one hand, nothing did happen at this spot, and yet on the other, something revolutionary happened. To stand here, is to stand where two titanic forces clashed. The ultimately victorious one would not jump to the dictates of any earthly power. Jesus knew his kingdom was not about catching the headlines but about obedience to the very end. To this day, it hard to stand there without being challenged by the radically antithetical way of the kingdom. However, there is something that makes this site doubly exciting. Quite possibly the place where Jesus did not jump was the place where the Holy Spirit fell!

Having stood at this corner for a time let's move on. Take a sharp ninety-degree turn to the left and before you lies a whole new archaeological park which has been opened up in recent years. You can see and walk up the impressive white stone steps that led up to the Gates of Huldah through which ancient visitors entered and exited the Temple Mount in the days of Jesus. To the south of the steps lies what would have been one of the largest open spaces in first century Jerusalem. Such large areas that could cope with an enormous crowd were rare in the city which would have been jammed with people at festival times. This area just south of the temple was particularly significant as it was a gathering point for pilgrims preparing to go into the Temple courts. Ritual baptismal chambers or 'mikvaot' dotted this area. Pilgrims who were ritually 'unclean', and so barred from the temple precincts, would have had to immerse themselves in these waters before entering 'the house' as the temple was often called. Priests would have witnessed their total immersion before declaring them ritually clean and therefore fit to enter the sacred mount. Is it possible that this was the actual location of the events of the Day of Pentecost?

Some recent scholarship makes a convincing case for this location. The geographical, archaeological and Biblical material harmonise in an exciting way. Firstly Luke records a crowd of at least three thousand who were gathered 'from every nation under heaven' (Acts 2:5 and 41). These 'God-fearing Jews' had come from all over the diaspora to the city for the annual celebration of Shavuot, or Weeks, one of three pilgrim feasts prescribed in the Torah. The festival takes its name from the fact that after Passover a period of seven weeks is counted off. '*Shavuot*' is simply the Hebrew word for 'weeks'. It is to state the obvious to say that seven weeks consist of forty-nine days but it is worth mentioning since the actual festival begins on the fiftieth day. The Greek word for fifty gives us 'Pentecost', a term we are all familiar with. Apart from this open space just south of the temple there were few places in the city where such a crowd could gather. Luke speaks of 'a sound like the blowing of a violent wind' that '*filled the whole house* where they were sitting' (Acts 2:2 emphasis mine). It is a known fact that the Jews often referred to the Temple as 'the house.' So the immediate context of the coming of the Holy Spirit was that of the celebration of a Torah-commanded harvest festival which drew thousands of Jews to the city and to the temple mount in particular. Just a few metres from the place where Jesus did not jump the Spirit fell upon the people with power. This new coming in power was nothing but a fulfilment of a promise that the Father had given sometime before. Jesus had instructed his disciples to 'wait for the gift my Father promised, which you have heard me speak about' (Acts 1:4). To better appreciate what he meant we shall enlist the aid of none other than Moses! The coming of that special gift on Pentecost marked a wish of Moses come true and the people experienced a divine presence that totally outshone that which had been in the Tent of Meeting which Moses had been commanded to build.

A wish come true for Moses.

In the Hebrew Bible, the Book of Numbers is known as '*Bamidbar*' which means 'in the wilderness'. In terms of reflecting the content of the fourth book of the Torah, this is a more accurate name. During those wilderness years Moses often had to cope with the moaning of the Israelites as they faced what they considered hardships. Quickly tiring of the manna that the

Lord had provided, they cried for meat. Their wailing drove Moses to distraction and not long into the desert he cried out to God, 'Why have you brought this trouble on your servant? What have I done to displease you that you have put the burden of all these people on me?' (Num. 11:11). Moses was ready to die rather than go on. He had had enough. It had become too much for him. In response, the Lord tells his servant that he would ease his burden by delegating seventy other men to share the responsibility of leadership. They would be anointed by the Holy Spirit specifically for their onerous task. Having reported this to the people, Moses 'brought together seventy of their elders and made them stand around the Tent. Then the Lord came down in the cloud and spoke with him, and he took of the Spirit that was on him and put the Spirit on the seventy elders. When the Spirit rested on them they prophesied, but they did not do so again' (Num. 11:24-25). This must have been like a prototype of Pentecost. However, to the great annoyance of Joshua, the Spirit also fell upon two other men outside the circle of the seventy. Joshua's immediate response was to order Moses to silence them, but Moses replied, 'Are you jealous for my sake? I wish that all the Lord's people were prophets, and the Lord would put his Spirit on them!' (Exod. 11:29-30). Moses would surely have rejoiced had he been able to see what Luke describes on the Day of Pentecost. Both men were talking about the same Spirit but one experienced only '*so much*', while the other, '*so much more*'. If the account in Numbers was about the Spirit coming on the seventy, then Acts was about the Spirit coming into the thousands. From Pentecost onwards the Spirit was not merely on, but in the people of God.

Absent in the body – present in the Spirit.

In the person of the Spirit, the Lord was present as never before. Surpassing the garden, tent, temple and even the flesh, the new presence was marked by an unprecedented fullness. Yet at the same time, it is worth asking if this is not what the Lord had intended from as early as his appearance on Mount Sinai. A close scrutiny of a Torah text through rabbinic eyes may prove very illuminating as we ponder an answer to this question.

We live in an age of verbal inflation. Words, like the money in our pockets, do not seem to go as far as they used to. The ancient Hebrews attached immeasurable value to words. The rabbis poured over the Scripture, savouring every word and counting every letter. They trawled through the text and often came up with tantalizing insights. One of their gems relates to the account of the Tent of Meeting. The text of Exodus gives us the account of the tent. God commands Moses to 'have them make a sanctuary for me, and I will dwell among them' (Exod. 25:8). The keen eye of an early Jewish commentator zooms in on the last two words. He observes the writer uses the plural pronoun *among them* and not a singular *in it* when referring to the sanctuary. In other words God's intention was not simply to live in a building in the neighbourhood but to actually live in the hearts of his own people. If the rabbis are correct in their insight then it would surely seem that the tent was second best to the human frame. A people, rather than simply a place, would have been the ideal for his presence. However, as he knocked at the door of their lives, the golden calf that Aaron had built was already in place in their innermost sanctuary. Surely the Lord would have wiped them out at this point had it not been for the intercessory mediation of Moses. In response to the pleas of Moses he promised them his presence in the tent. The intimate reality of God dwelling in the very lives of his people would have to await the coming of a new age. That is precisely what happened at Pentecost. The God who came down at Sinai to dwell in a tent, now came in Jerusalem to dwell in the lives of his people. Jesus had returned to heaven so that the Spirit would come in fulfilment of the Father's promise. The presence that had been localised in the tent, temple and body had now become universalised. Jesus had left the earth in a body but had now returned in the Spirit. What 'Jesus began to do and to teach until the day he was taken up to heaven' (Acts 1:1-2), he now continues to do in the Spirit. Perhaps we would be better to rename the 'Acts of the Apostles' as the 'Ongoing Acts of Jesus in the Spirit'.

While the Spirit had been active at creation and throughout the history of Israel, the fullness of his coming at Pentecost was such that John could even say at one point 'up to that time the Spirit had not been given, since Jesus had not been glorified' (John 7:29). It defies belief to suggest John would have been ignorant of the Spirit of God in the history of God's dealings with Israel. The Spirit hovered over the act of creation, empowered prophets and inspired poets. Most certainly he would have known of this but now he wants to make a point forcefully. John is thinking in relative terms. He is comparing one age with another age. What had gone before was so little in comparison to what had come as a result of Jesus. Yes, the Spirit had been there all along but his significance was as nothing in comparison to what it would be with his coming after the glorification of Jesus. God's presence in the flesh had been real, but localised. His presence in the Spirit meant he was no longer confined to one body or one place. Now his presence could be experienced anywhere on the face of the earth. As he had promised the Samaritan woman at the well, 'the time is coming and has now come when the true worshippers will worship the Father in spirit and truth' (John 4:23). The location for true worship is not merely in Jerusalem, Rome, Canterbury or Geneva but in the Spirit. The presence of God is now in his people. Jesus did not leave behind a building but a body of people in whom his Spirit dwells. While present in the flesh he promised never to abandon his own. By way of reassurance he affirmed that he would ask his Father 'and he will give you another Counsellor to be with you for ever – the Spirit of truth. The world cannot accept him, because it neither sees him nor knows him, for he lives with you and will be in you. I will not leave you as orphans; I will come to you'(John 14:16-18). He was about to come to dwell in a radically different sanctuary.

Construction of the new temple commenced with the unique and dramatic events recorded in the opening chapters of Acts. Indicating the nature of this new dwelling place of God, Paul wrote to the Corinthians, 'Don't you know that you yourselves are God's temple and that God's Spirit lives in you?'(1 Cor. 3:16). On both an individual and a corporate level 'we are the temple of the living God'(2 Cor. 6:16 see also 1 Cor. 6:19). Furthermore, to underline his point, he actually quotes a striking verse from Leviticus in justification of his assertion. Schooled in Torah, he highlighted the fact that 'God has said: "I will live with them and walk among them, and I will be their God and they will be my people"(2 Cor. 6:16). Unlike a modern reader, the first readers of Paul would have known the context of this quotation and it would not have been lost on them that in the preceding verse in Leviticus, God had promised 'I will put my dwelling place among you, and I will not abhor you'(Lev. 26:11). Ordinary believers are now 'like living stones...being built into a spiritual house to be a holy priesthood offering spiritual sacrifices acceptable to God through Jesus Christ' (1 Pet. 2:5). All is focused on Christ for 'in him the whole building is joined together and rises to become a holy temple in the Lord. And in him you too are being built together to become a dwelling in which God lives by his Spirit' (Eph. 2:21-22). This is surely one of the most amazing building projects that has ever been seen on the face of the earth. Moreover, it is ongoing. Greater than any of the ancient or modern wonders of the world, a spiritual house is being built by God and 'we are his house, if we hold on to our courage and the hope of which we boast' (Heb. 3:6). At the heart of all this activity is the Holy Spirit.

Climactic though this coming of the Spirit may have been, it really only marked the start of something even much bigger. The arrival of the Spirit was an integral part of the complex of events that marked the end of the Old Covenant but it also inaugurated the beginning of the last days of the world as we know it.

Beginning of the end – firstfruits of the Spirit.

When the role of the Spirit is discussed in Christian circles, the conversation is all too often limited to how he relates to the individual believer. Later on, we shall return to look at that aspect of his work but before that we need to get back into the shuttle and zoom way out for a bigger picture. In preceding chapters we have focused in on the tent in the desert, the temple in Jerusalem and the person of Jesus but now we go into orbit again. This time you will probably feel the gravitational forces at work. In this section I am going to invite you to think outside your normal box but inside the triangle!

When grappling with a big idea, I have always found it helpful to reduce it to the degree that I can get some sort of hold of it. That is where simple diagrams come to my aid. Of course, I am not suggesting that Biblical truth can be reduced to geometric drawings on a page, but perhaps we can learn something from the political cartoonist who can take complex issues and express them graphically with a few pen strokes. So what follows is neither about geometry nor cartoons, but a tentative attempt to grasp some big issues with a few simple strokes. We shall build our picture step by step. Our model consists of two simple triangles which represent two separate ages.

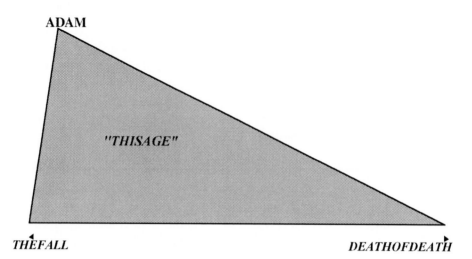

ADAM

"THISAGE"

THEFALL   *DEATHOFDEATH*

The first triangle represents what the Jews, including therefore Jesus and Paul, called 'this age' or 'this world'. The base can be used as a time line indicating the sweep from the fall of Adam to the final destruction of the last enemy, namely death, at a point that is still in the future for us. As your finger follows that bottom line from left to right, your mind hurtles through time as you begin in Genesis and look beyond Revelation. Now you see what I mean when I say that we are about to think on a big scale. World history is being condensed onto a paperback page! There is not a book big enough to hold this material.

Not only does the triangle help us to be expansive but it enables us to be inclusive. One of the most obvious things about a triangle is that there is an apex. Our eye is naturally drawn to the vertex. This single point at the top helps us focus on the one person who represents this whole age. Standing boldly on this tip is Adam. In this one man all of humanity is concentrated. He is the one who represents the many. Such thinking is alien to our modern western individualism. but deeply characteristic of the Hebrew mind. Paul gives us a clear example when he asserts 'sin entered the world through one man, and death through sin, and in this way death came to all men, because all sinned' (Rom. 5:12 emphasis added). Evidently the apostle understood the many were represented in the one. Adam was an individual but also a representative individual. In the divinely appointed scheme of things he acted in total identity and solidarity with the rest of humanity.

The clash of David and Goliath provides us with a fascinating insight into this principle at work on a different scale.. Most people are familiar with the story of the young Jewish shepherd boy confronting the Philistine giant with a sling. What I never could grasp was why the Philistines did not sweep down and defeat the Israelites after the totally unexpected defeat of their giant Goliath. The evidence suggests that militarily they were actually superior and much better equipped. In those days the Philistines had a virtual monopoly on iron and so had better weapons. Even the Israelites had to go down to their neighbours to get their ploughshares sharpened. Unquestionably Goliath was a big loss in more ways than one, but the Philistines still had the superior hand. Their acceptance of defeat is virtually incomprehensible apart from this concept of representation or corporate personality. What both camps understood perfectly was that David's victory was a victory for all whom he represented and Goliath's defeat was a defeat for all whom he represented. Neither man had stood by or for himself. So Adam did not act as a mere individual. He acted as the representative of humanity and ' the result of *one trespass* was *condemnation for all men*, ...through the disobedience of *the one man the many* were made sinners' (Rom. 8:18-19 emphasis added). One man's act of disobedience issued in an age dominated by wrath, sin, law and death. 'This present evil age' (Gal. 1:4) is marked by decay, evil, frustration and vanity. Paul also refers to it as *'this world'* (Rom. 12:2) with its own 'wisdom'(1 Cor. 2:6). Jesus, too, speaks of 'the sons of *this age* (Luke 20:34). This is a dark place to be. This is what we are born into. The deeper our awareness of the darkness, the brighter will be our understanding of the gospel. The more we sense death, the greater our wonder about rebirth. The more powerful our sense of the horror of this first age, then the greater our hope in what burst into this with the coming of Christ and the dawn of the new age.

Our second triangle represents the bursting in of another age. In time, this new age is consecutive with the old, in scope, as comprehensive as the old but in meaning, totally antithetical to the old. Once again, the base can serve as a time-line. This time it commences the coming of Jesus. In the diagram the cross is a simple way of indicating the entirety of the Christ event, namely his birth, ministry, death, resurrection, ascension and his

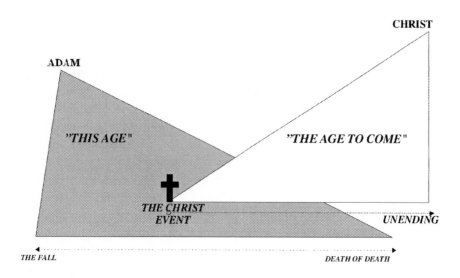

sending of the Spirit. This complex of events encompassing Christmas to Pentecost inaugurates the new and final age in God's plan. This time as our fingers follow the line we shall go off the page and our minds are projected into the eternal future. We begin with the Gospels, move through Acts and the Pauline letters into Revelation and beyond. Kingdom history takes us well off the page!

At the apex of the first triangle there stands a man, so too, one governs the second. Where once Adam ruled, now Christ reigns. What Adam ruined, Christ redeemed. The ruin that came through disobedience is countered by the redemption that came through obedience. Paul draws the contrast vividly. For 'if *the many* died by the trespass of *the one man*, how much more did God's grace and the gift that came by the grace of *the one man*, Jesus Christ, overflow to *the many!*' (Rom. 5:15 emphasis added). The contrast between these two triangles could not be greater. They represent a titanic clash. Incidentally, from a fictional perspective, J.R.R.Tolkein's famous trilogy, '*The Lord of the Rings*' gives the reader a wonderful sense of the proportions of this clash of good and evil. Jesus' entry to our world was an engagement with powers of darkness. War was launched against a darkness that had been entrenched since the days of Adam. Yet at precisely the point where those powers of evil seemed victorious, namely the cross, God the Father would show his power by raising Jesus from the dead. By his death and resurrection, Jesus ushered in the new age. 'The time had fully come' (Gal. 4:4). As Simeon took the child Jesus he knew that '*now*' salvation had come and into the darkness shone 'a light for revelation to the Gentiles and for glory to your people Israel' (Luke 2:32). Paul knew the long awaited day of salvation had dawned (2 Cor. 6:2). The writer of Hebrews had an equally cosmic perspective when he said Christ 'has appeared once for all at the end of the ages to do away with sin by the sacrifice of himself' (Heb. 9:26). When we strip the tinsel off Christmas, then we really see what it was about. It was the launching of a series of events that marked the bursting in of the long-awaited *age to come*. Messiah had arrived. The beginning of the end had come. Parenthetically, we observe that many Jewish people still await the dawning of the *age to come*. Christians, who acknowledge Jesus as the long-awaited Jewish Messiah, obviously regard his coming as the beginning of the whole new order of things. An integral part of that new order is the Holy Spirit. The coming of the Spirit is inseparable from the coming of Jesus.

What is immediately obvious in the diagram that we have been using is the overlap of the two triangles. On the one hand the *age to come* is already here but on the other hand it is not yet here fully. Along with every believer since the apostolic age we live in that overlap of the ages. Around us is the presence of that old age but within us the reality of whole dynamic. Within is the presence of the Spirit of the new age that dawned with Christ.

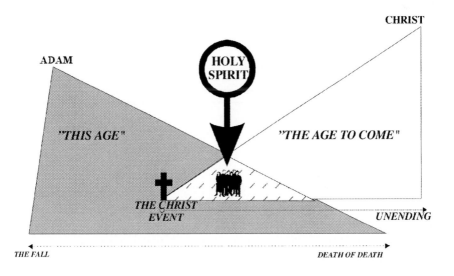

Paul communicates this extraordinary reality by means of two wonderfully vivid images. To the Corinthians he says God 'anointed us, set his seal of ownership on us, and put his Spirit in our hearts as *a deposit*, guaranteeing what is to come'(2 Cor. 1:22 emphasis added). Then to the Romans he makes the same point but uses a farming image, when he affirms 'we ourselves,...have the *firstfruits* of the Spirit' (Rom. 8:23). Both images reflect the robust concreteness of Hebraic thought. Paul paints vivid word pictures on the canvas of his listeners' ears. Both 'deposit' and 'firstfruits' are pregnant with meaning. On the surface they are simple and accessible to all, yet there is such profundity that they can be mined for deeper significance.

Both words offer certainty. The deposit is known the world over as a way of indicating a serious commitment and the guarantee that payment in full will follow. Similarly for the farmer, the firstfruits were an indication that the crop had started to mature and that this was first of a much bigger harvest that would follow in time. Common to both images is the waiting period between the initial and the final. Something has started and will be completed.

To appreciate what Paul is saying we need to move from the micro to the macro level. Yes, he says, the Spirit has come, the new age has dawned but what we have now is not the fullness but simply the firstfruits or the deposit. In other words God has started something and we can be sure he will complete it because that is his nature. However we find ourselves in the waiting room. It is not easy to wait and sometimes we get very edgy. When all around does not seem to make sense then we need to remind ourselves that God has not finished yet. Pentecost was God's way of saying that he was serious. Something much bigger started on that day and it has not been completed yet. As believers, we must live with a wait on our minds. However, the wait is eased by the knowledge that God always finishes what he starts. The Son came and the Spirit came so, too, the end will come. Until that day the Spirit is within the people of God as a sort of heavenly homing device. His presence makes us restive, making us 'groan inwardly as we wait eagerly for adoption as sons, the redemption of our bodies. For in this hope we were saved. But hope that is seen is no hope at all. Who hopes for what he already has? But if we hope for what we do not yet have, we wait for it patiently. In the same way, the Spirit helps us in our weakness' (Rom. 8:23-26). It is good to remember that in our weakness we now live in the power sphere of the Spirit. The believer is now part of a whole new order of things. Where death was once regnant, the Spirit now rules.

Dead to the world – living in the Spirit

In Christ, we have died to the old age and now live under a new power. On the cross, not only Christ, but all whom he represented died to the old order of things. By means of his death, rebirth became a reality. The drama is captured by Paul when he exclaims 'if anyone is in Christ, he is a new creation; the old has gone, the new has come!' (2 Cor. 5:17). In terms of our diagram, we move from one triangle into the other! While this is exciting beyond words, there is more to it than mere emotion. Biblical images of this transfer abound. The dead live, the blind see, the orphan is adopted and the slave is freed. To grasp the sheer wonder of this transition, and subsequent transformation, we need to see it on both the subjective and objective level.

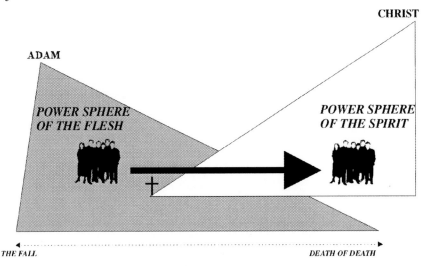

CHRIST

ADAM

POWER SPHERE OF THE FLESH

POWER SPHERE OF THE SPIRIT

THE FALL   *DEATH OF DEATH*

I often liken the transition from the one age to the other to someone taking on a new nationality. For instance, a British person living in New York may decide to become an American citizen. After all the legalities, the new citizen of the United States of America walks out with his or her citizenship papers. A few days later, our new American citizen turns on the television only to hear Elgar's 'Pomp and Circumstance'. Suddenly that old British identity swells up inside and mentally he or she is standing waving a Union Jack outside Buckingham Palace. Subjectively, the passion for the old allegiance is stirred up, but objectively, the fact is that the new citizen is now subject to new authority. The old regime has no power over him or her. On the subjective level there may be an intense struggle with emotions but on the objective level there is an irrefutable fact. The old order has gone! Christians need to be reminded of this at times. They live in the environment of the old age but the objective reality is that in Christ they are under a totally new sovereign power. In our final chapter we shall explore how this relates to both sin and death but for now we see the believer is no longer 'in Adam' but 'in Christ' and under the rule of the Spirit. Both the coming and the work of the Spirit are inseparable from the coming and work of Jesus.

So far in this chapter we have been thinking in cosmic terms. I promised you that we would begin to think outside the proverbial box. Hopefully those triangles have given us a new perspective on eschatology. Perhaps they help to impress on us the reality of the beginning of the end. The Son and the Spirit have come. The last days have started and people like you and me are part of this final stage of God's plan. Now, we are going to be more personal. It would be tempting to ignore the big picture because it is daunting in its complexity and scale. It is all too easy to give up on the cosmic dimension and to feel content in our own little corner. However, the 'Jesus and me' type of personal faith is best made sense of in the context of God and the cosmos. Knowing where I am, and who I am, in the big picture gives meaning to what I can do for the Lord. At one and the same time it is humbling and uplifting to grasp how the Spirit is at work in the individual.

Accomplished by the Son – applied by the Spirit.

Melody Green did not sacrifice depth for the sake of clarity when she wrote,

> *Thank You, O my Father,*
> *for giving us Your Son,*
> *and leaving Your Spirit*
> *till the work on earth is done.*
> (Melody Green, Word Music,UK, Mission Praise,673)

The mystery of Trinitarian relationships provides the backdrop for the wonder of the Spirit's ongoing task in our world. The Creator God who is above us is the Father; the Redeeming God who was with us is the Son; the transforming God who now is within us is the Holy Spirit. Only one God, creating, redeeming and sanctifying.

While the *'age to come'* may have burst into history the work of God is not complete. What God had accomplished in Christ, he continues to apply in the Spirit. While Jesus completed the task that he had been given, that act of salvation which he finished continues to be worked out in lives today by his Spirit. To reflect on how the Spirit is active in the lives of individuals is to explore what we might call 'the inside story'. What the Spirit does is not always visible. In fact, as an agent he is invisible to the human eye. He works rather like the wind. It is no surprise to find that the Hebrew word for spirit is also the word for 'wind'. As Jesus himself once said, 'The wind blows wherever it pleases. You hear its sound, but you cannot tell where it comes from or where it is going. So it is with everyone born of the Spirit' (John 4:8). Centuries later R.L.Stevenson wrote in his own inimitable style about the wind, and what he says to children may well prove helpful to adults thinking about deeper issues. Perhaps I may do him an injustice by reading in my own interpretation, but on first reading 'The Wind' I kept thinking about the Spirit's modus operandi. Here he introduces the wind.

> *I saw you toss the kites on high*
> *And blow the birds about the sky;*
> *And all around I heard you pass,*
> *Like ladies' skirts across the grass—*
> *O wind a-blowing all day long,*
> *O wind, that sings so loud a song!*

But it is the next verse that I find eminently appropriate when applied to the working of the Spirit.

I saw the different things you did,
But always you yourself you hid.
I felt you push, I heard you call
I could not see yourself at all—
O wind a-blowing all day long,
O wind, that sings so loud a song!

There is nothing ostentatious about the Spirit's activity. Yet while he is invisible he is also invincible. As the chief executive of the Godhead, he has boundless power and touches the lives of many throughout the world. Present at the creation of the world, who is better placed to be active in the new creation that takes place in the life of a believer? One of the most decidedly interesting features of the Biblical record is that the very same Spirit who 'was hovering over the waters' in the creation account (Gen. 1:2) descended on Mary at the commencement of the new creation. The angel announced to the village virgin, 'The Holy Spirit will come upon you and the power of the Most High will overshadow you'(Luke 1:33). Luke links the two beginnings in a quite dramatic way. On both the cosmic and personal levels the Spirit is at work. At one and the same time, Mary is both unique and representative in her experience of the Spirit. She is unique in being the virgin who gave birth to the Son of God at a specific time in history. Yet she is also representative in the sense that the new life within her was not the fruit of human activity. To this very day, any of us who experience the reality of new life within know that this is a result of a divine intervention. Whether in the case of Mary, or in our situation, the life within is the fruit of both Spirit and Word in a dynamic relationship. Over two millennia after he visited Mary, the Spirit still enters ordinary lives to bring new life and inaugurate a whole new order of things.

This source of new life is also the agent of inner cleansing and promoter of holy living. Having been born into, and lived much of life in the old age, every believer needs to be spiritually (and sometimes physically) detoxified. There are former patterns of behaviour and thought that need to be removed from our system. As Paul pointed out to the early Roman believers 'if you live according to the sinful nature, you will die; but if by the Spirit you put to death the misdeeds of the body, you will live, because those who are led by the Spirit of God are sons of God' (Rom. 8:13-14). Paradoxically the life-giving Spirit puts to death what belongs to the old earthly nature, namely 'sexual immorality, impurity, lust, evil desires and greed' (Col. 3:5). Both around us and within us, this present age battles on with a tenacity we dare not minimize. We may have been reborn to a new status in the age to come but until Christ's rule is total we have a struggle on our hands. This is a battle we shall return to in the final chapter as we seek to explore how we relate to both sin and death in the present moment.

As the Spirit engages with everything that is unworthy within us, he also affirms us in our new citizenship or family membership. He dispels fear as he 'testifies with our spirit that we are God's children' (Rom. 8:16). He answers to the deep-seated need to belong that is within us all. Irrespective of our experiences with earthly fathers, some of whom may have fallen far short of the ideal, the Spirit binds us in a loving relationship to our heavenly Father. At the same time he cements the family ties among Christians and points beyond the 'hour' to the 'our' of salvation. In the Spirit, oriental and occidental, northerner and southerner, black and white, male and female, young and old, educated and uneducated, married and unmarried, republican and monarchist are bound together in a love that transcends all other differences.

Diversity of gifts – unity in the Spirit.

Some years ago a senior figure in the MacDonald's fast food chain pointed out what he believed to be one of the major reasons why burger sales had burgeoned. He claimed that the fundamental secret under the golden arches was that they had achieved uniformity and allegiance to one operating regime without sacrificing the strengths of individualism and diversity. In other words conformity coexisted with creativity. Perhaps the church needs to take note. If this was the secret to selling burgers could it not be used in distributing the bread of life? The fact is, Paul had been advocating this very principle long before the MacDonald brothers had pushed out their handcart.

In Paul's picture of the church, total loyalty to one Lord was not at the expense of individual creativity. Making this very point he shows a sense of humour that still brings a smile to the modern face. What better model of unity and diversity at work than that of the human body. With a wry humour Paul points this out to the Corinthian church. Firstly he establishes 'the body is a unity, though it is made up of many parts; and though all its parts are many, they form one body. So it is with Christ. For we were all baptised by one Spirit into one body – whether Jews or Greeks, slave or free – and we were all given one Spirit to drink' (1 Cor. 12:12-13). Nonetheless, what would be patently absurd in my body is only too often a reality in the church. How could we function if our foot refused to work simply because it was not a hand? Paul invites us to eavesdrop on 'Body Talk!' – a satire in one act depicting the church . First on stage is the foot. Emotionally he feels that he has been trampled. Because he is not a hand he has concluded that he is useless and does not even belong. The ear now joins the chorus lamenting that because he is not an eye he has no part in the body either. The parody could go on as each part of the body rubbishes itself because it is not something or someone else. The scene would be hilarious were it not so tragically true in the church. How many people feel that because they are not someone else or that they cannot do something else then it follows that they are worthless? Yet withal, the very diversity that they conclude makes them worthless, is what actually gives them worth in the body of Christ. Like the parts of the body in the Pauline parody, they are correct in affirming that they are different, but they are wrong in deducing that this difference means they are inferior or useless. Their strength lies in that individuality. 'If the whole body were an ear where would the sense of smell be? But in fact God has arranged the parts of the body, every one of them, just as he wanted them to be. If they were all one part, where would the body be? As it is, there are many parts, but one body' (1 Cor. 12:17-20).

Paul's analogy also highlights that what is obviously natural in my body is only too often forced and artificial in the church. When I am healthy, I never seem to stop to think about the various organs that are functioning day in and out. Some things just seem to go on whether or not I am conscious of them. I enjoy my food but never consciously stop to will my digestive system to work. In the morning, I rise refreshed after a sleep during which I never once willed my breathing to continue. A lot just seems to happen in the healthy body. However sore spots do tend to draw inordinate attention to themselves when they need attention. I sometimes wonder what it would be like if the church as the Body of Christ functioned more naturally. What if evangelism, like our breathing, became a regular feature of life rather than a sporadic gasp or a special event to draw in new life? What if social action became a natural movement that we engaged in without even thinking? Hands reach out to the needy and help steady the faltering as a matter of course. Backs and knees bend easily to bring us down to the level of the fallen. Healthy parts of the body draw little attention to themselves but work away for the good of the whole. The Spirit is at work in the whole body and the ordinary can be as much a testimony to that reality as the extraordinary. Too often today, hunger for the miraculous blinds us to God at work in the mundane. He is often at work in the course of the ordinary. He can take our capacities, even perhaps aptitudes that we had before conversion, and bring them under the controlling power of divine grace, using them in the service of the kingdom of God.

Jesus did walk on water but he also used boats. Jesus raised a girl from the dead but he asked her parents to fetch her some food. So, too, we find that the Spirit does not work in ostentatious ways. He is not a showman. He did not come for the shelf or the self. God did not send him as a trophy to be boasted about and displayed on a shelf. Nor did he give him for the personal indulgence of any individual who would only glory in a personal experience. He came for the communal good of the church. Never should the individual blind us to the community, nor the extraordinary eclipse the ordinary.

To some, who were in danger of boasting too much of their personal experience, Paul issues a word of warning that the edification of the church is more important than personal pride in the exercise of gifts. He counselled the Corinthians, 'I would like everyone of you to speak in tongues, but I would rather have you prophesy. He who prophesies is greater than the one who speaks in tongues, unless he interprets, so that the church may be edified' (1 Cor. 14:5). At the heart of such edification there is no more powerful combination than the Spirit of God in harmony with the Word of God.

Word of the Lord – Sword of the Spirit.

While the pages of church history sadly record so much tension between the Spirit and the Word of God, the pages of Scripture open with a wonderful picture of a creative and harmonious relationship between the two. The opening scene is dramatic. The Spirit hovers. Incidentally the modern Hebrew word for hovercraft is derived from the verb describing the Spirit's activity in Genesis. It is under this all-pervasive presence that the word is spoken. The dynamic and creative power of the word is thus inseparable from the brooding presence of the Spirit. What a picture! Spirit and Word working in perfect harmony.

Earlier in this chapter we drew attention to Mary's experience marking the beginning of the work of new creation, but Pentecost also affords us an opportunity to explore an often overlooked marriage between Spirit and Word. While Christians associate Pentecost with the gift of the Holy Spirit, Jews celebrate Shavuot as marking the gift of the Torah. In Jewish tradition Shavuot or Weeks has an agricultural significance marking the firstfruits of the barley harvest but it has also been given a historical meaning inasmuch as it commemorates the giving of the Torah at Sinai. While the tongues of fire are symbolic of the Spirit for the Christian, they are evocations of Sinai for the Jew. There, the encounter between God and Israel had been a defining moment. Led by Moses, the people had gone 'out of the camp to meet with God, and they stood at the foot of the mountain. Mount Sinai was covered with smoke, because the Lord descended on it in fire' (Exod. 19:17-18). Centuries later, the God who had come down in fire on Sinai Mount now revealed himself again at the Temple Mount. To this day, Jews celebrate the giving of Torah at the festival of Shavuot. Just exactly when they began to link the giving of Torah with this feast is uncertain, but that they do affords us an opportunity to explore further the relationship between Spirit and Word and perhaps between Christian and Jew. One of the fascinating traditions in Jerusalem is that religious Jews stay up all night to study Torah and then at dawn make their way to join the crowds praying at the Western Wall. Such scenes are still powerfully evocative of that Pentecost event when the Spirit came upon the waiting mass of people gathered at 'the house'. What a cause for celebration! What an exciting opportunity to explore once more the harmony of Spirit and Word. The God who had come down from the mountain top to dwell in the midst of his people was now present as never before. The tent was only a memory as the Spirit now lived in a human frame. Yet there is no 'happy ever after' to conclude the Pentecost story. Quite the opposite is true. Where the Spirit is there is a restless groaning. No one in whom the Spirit dwells can live with the status quo. The Spirit who had been present at creation cannot live with things as they are now. Indeed, 'we know that the whole creation has been groaning as in the pains of childbirth right up to the present time. Not only so, but we ourselves, who have the firstfruits of the Spirit, groan inwardly as we wait eagerly'(Rom. 8:22-23). Yes, the Spirit has come but there is still more to come.

Chapter 6

In the New Jerusalem

"They'll shut the motorway!"

One wintry night I was driving home from Belfast. I had just joined the motorway and had started to accelerate when my eye was drawn to what appeared to be a field of sparkling diamonds. The ground was sprinkled with fallen stars vying with each other to be the most dazzling. The effect was hypnotic. It seemed totally surreal. It was as if light was bursting out of the ground. Then it dawned on me. Off to my right was one of the biggest cemeteries in the city and the passing headlights were simply being refracted by the headstones. So it was not something extra-terrestrial after all. Nonetheless, it kick-started my imagination to explore what it will be like on the coming day when the dead will be raised.

The next day I was describing the experience to a group of students. I was explaining how the incident prompted me to think of what Jesus said about the graves opening and the dead being raised. After waxing lyrical on great eschatological events predicted in Scripture for a few minutes, I concluded with what I intended as a rhetorical question. "What will be it be like at the coming resurrection?" With that profound thought I thought the conversation was over, but with the speed of an Intel processor a student shot back, "Desi, they'll shut the motorway!" Indeed they will.

In fact, I got to wondering as we approach the end of our journey that has brought us from the Garden of Eden to this particular point in the book, what can we say about the climax that is coming? Probably the best vantage point to view this from is within the city that John describes as coming down from heaven. In the final chapters of Scripture, John leaves us with an astounding vision of 'the new Jerusalem, coming down out of heaven from God'

(Rev. 21:2). He saw 'a new heaven and a new earth, for the first heaven and the first earth had passed away' (Rev. 21:1). To mark the end of our pilgrimage through the great plan of redemptive revelation we are going to try to get something of a glimpse from that city. This is the final place we shall meet God revealing himself. He has been in the garden, tent, temple, flesh and presently with us in the Spirit, but the new city is his final abode. At our most daring we can only take a few tentative steps towards imagining what it will be like. This book began with something of a challenge to try to think our way into the world before the fall. It is no easy task to picture creation in its pristine, sinless perfection. Now, as the book comes to a conclusion, let's engage that sanctified imagination once more. This time, we are going to attempt to project ourselves into the city that John sees coming down from above. In this final chapter, I invite you to join me as we stand somewhere in that new city, and from that vantage point lift up our hands in praise to God for what he has done. We shall be given an unprecedented view over his purposes and how they have been worked out. We shall see as we have never seen before with both the eyes in our head and the eyes in our heart. We shall be in the phenomenally privileged position where there will be no more waiting, no more death, no more pain, no more brokenness and no more temple.

However, before exploring the future we need to understand the past. Central to the whole plan of God is Jesus Christ. His person and work are pivotal in the overall plan that we are tracing. Nobody realises that more keenly than John in the last book of the Bible. The New Jerusalem is unimaginable apart from Christ's perfect fulfilment of the plan.

No more waiting – the plan is now complete.

Messiah's coming was central to the hope of Israel. Down through the centuries the messianic hope grew, and for a moment we want to try to think our way into the mind of an expectant Jew living in the days of the old covenant. During those centuries anticipation focused on the promised one to come. Messiah's advent would bring an end to *this age* and launch the '*age to come*'.

Messiah's coming

THIS AGE	AGE TO COME

It is easy to see that the arrival of Messiah marked the ultimate watershed between the two ages. Earlier in the book we alluded to the fact that many Jews, who do not see Jesus as Messiah, are still waiting for the coming event. The death of Rabbi Menachem Mendel Schneerson in 1994 affords a fascinating example of this. Rabbi Schneerson, known to his followers as the *'Rebbe'*, was the leader of a traditional Orthodox group known as the Lubavitchers. Born in Europe, he fled to North America in 1941 and spent the remainder of his days in Brooklyn, New York. During his lifetime he was instrumental in founding a worldwide network of institutions for study and he brought messianism to the forefront of the Jewish world. As he surveyed the fall of communism and the events of the Gulf War, he said that these were the signs of a coming time of peace and tranquility for humanity. In other words, they were heralding the time of Messiah. Within his own community, many actually regarded him as the Messiah, but this contention was disputed in the wider Jewish world. Nonetheless, when he died in June 1994 thousands of sorrowing but expectant followers descended on New York. El Al even put on extra flights. Many flocked to the Big Apple in the belief that he would rise again as Messiah and bring in the age of peace.

Christians have a radically different perspective. Like the Jews, we believe in the two age scheme of history, but unlike them we affirm that Messiah has come, and with Jesus the *'age to come'* has already started. In fact we are already over two thousand years into the last days. Like the Apostle Paul, we affirm the reality of the two-age scheme and adjust it to the fact that Messiah's coming is actually in two stages. It never entered the mind of the people waiting under the old covenant that the coming of Messiah would actually involve two stages. The incarnation would mark his coming in humility, but then he would return in glory. The implication of this is radical. With the coming of Jesus the *age to come* burst into world history. His kingdom had come, but not yet fully. Since his coming, the ages overlap. Incidentally, this is simply another perspective on the overlap we saw with the two triangles.

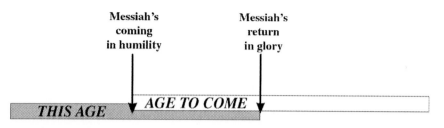

So the good news is that the *age to come* has begun; the even better news is that there is more to come when Jesus returns: death is destroyed and the Lord will rule over all. With the return of Jesus, the last enemy, namely death, is conquered absolutely. The end of death marks the end of the old age. Jesus' return is the completion of what he commenced. Perhaps you are already asking how this fits in with your eschatology. You are reading this, as indeed I am writing this, using the spectacles we have acquired over the years. We all wear them. They are called presuppositions. Through reading and preaching many of us have some perception of the events of the last times. My purpose here is not to enter into the arguments for and against various eschatologies which may be sincerely held. Rather than defend one against the others, I want to focus on the significance of Christ's return and not simply the timetable. What really counts is his victory and not our formulae. God did not attach a fold-out sheet to the back cover of the Bible, detailing the dates. From the perspective of cosmic history his two comings are really inseparable. Ultimately they combine to make one great Messianic event. As we survey the big picture from our seat in the shuttle cockpit we are struck by one stupendous event, namely the coming of Messiah.

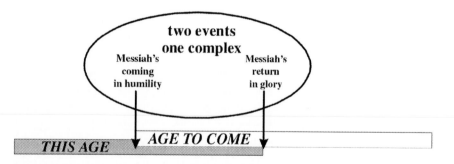

This is not an easy thing for us to take in, since we have to grapple with the fact that, to date, over two millennia have passed since his first appearance.

However, we are trying to see God's plan from a cosmic, not a personal perspective. The words spoken through Isaiah are particularly appropriate. As the Lord said 'my thoughts are not your thoughts, neither are your ways my ways…as the heavens are higher than the earth, so are my ways higher than your ways and my thoughts than your thoughts' (Isa. 55:8-9). Or as the Psalmist observes, 'a thousand years in your (God's) sight are like a day that has just gone by' (Ps. 90:4). What a different perspective that gives us on time!

At the moment, we are still in the waiting room, but what gives us confidence is the assurance that what he has started is real and cannot be stopped. Despite the mind-blowing scale of this scheme, I hope, at the very least, to have made it clear that we are now living in apocalyptic times. Life between the comings is demanding but exciting. Now is a time for us to be active in God's service, now is the day of salvation. Our faith is set in the context of God's great plan coming to a conclusion. Every believer is part of an apocalyptic people. No matter how small or insignificant we may be tempted to feel, the reality is that we are all involved in a much bigger plan. From the perspective of the New Jerusalem we shall look back and celebrate the completion of the plan in which Christ was the central figure and the conqueror of the last enemy.

No more death – the old order is now gone.

There will be no funeral homes or cemeteries in this new city that John sees. There will be no death notices or obituaries in the newspapers. Death will have been banished for ever. Death will have died. That is a big claim in a short sentence, but John could not be clearer in his assertion that 'there will be no more death or mourning or crying or pain, for the old order of things has passed away' (Rev. 21:4).

Even though we know that Christ died and rose again victorious over the power of death, we still suffer from its sting. In a previous chapter we established that while the Christ event was momentous, it still only ushered in the new age, but did not consummate it. The coming of Jesus and the subsequent gift of the Spirit marked the beginning of the end, but what John is now talking about is the end of that beginning. John's vision is of the absolute end. If John could see our imaginary triangles, then he would be

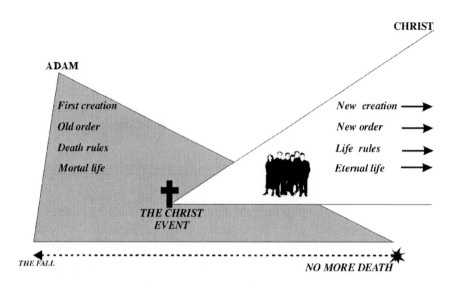

CHRIST

ADAM

First creation
Old order
Death rules
Mortal life

New creation ⟶
New order ⟶
Life rules ⟶
Eternal life ⟶

THE CHRIST EVENT

THE FALL   *NO MORE DEATH*

saying the overlap is gone! For him the old age is not just starting to go, it has gone. And when did it start to go? Perhaps you think that I am being repetitive, but it is so crucial that we all grasp that final push started with Jesus coming, dying and rising on the earth.

To deliver us from the old state, Christ had to identify with our human condition. We are going to survey how he related to and then changed our state in a dramatic way. Having done that in terms of four identifiable steps, we shall then explore two ways in which the Bible describes what has happened to us. Firstly, we shall use the rather unusual model of circumcision to see how we have been cut off from an old way of life, and then, secondly, the image of creation to depict how we have been included in a new way of life.

If you get sentimental about Christmas as it is observed by modern western society, then you need to brace yourself for what is coming. When Jesus was born, Bethlehem was not lit up like tinsel town, but lay in the darkness of an age dominated by the merciless totalitarian regimes of law, sin and death. Such was the world he entered. His birth was the launch of a campaign against alien powers that stood in opposition to God. Humanity, without exception and without excuse, was in a state of sin, far short of the glory of God (Rom. 3:23). While God's law served to highlight the reality and nature of that state, it actually exacerbated the problem at the same time, in as much as it

86

could convict, but not save the sinner. The Apostle Paul wrestles with this at some length in his Letter to the Romans. Deftly he describes and probes the nature of life in this age as one of both hopelessness and helplessness under the merciless triumvirate of sin, law and death. Only a gracious initiative in the form of a divine intrusion could save the situation.

The human condition	Jesus identifies with our condition	By his death, Jesus breaks the power of	'In Christ' believers are freed from
under sin	made to be sin	Sin	Sin
under law	born under law	Law	Law
under death	subjected to death	Death	Death

Schematically the first column outlines the human tragedy but in the second column we have the beginning of the divine strategy. God was not going to save humanity from a distance. Christmas was about solidarity. When Israel had been in tents, the Lord was in a tent; when they settled in houses of stone, the Lord was in a temple, but the ultimate expression of solidarity came when he took on a body. 'Since the children have flesh and blood, he too shared in their humanity so that by his death he might destroy him who holds the power of death – that is, the devil – and free those who all their lives were held in slavery by their fear of death. For surely it is not angels he helps, but Abraham's descendant. For this reason he had to be made like his brothers in every way, in order that he might become a merciful and faithful high priest in service to God, and that he might make atonement for the sins of the people' (Heb. 2:14-17).

The first Christmas was primarily about presence rather than presents. In Christ, God had come onto our plane. He came to walk where we walk and, remarkably, be tempted as we are tempted yet remain sinless himself. The Book of Hebrews expresses the extent of his identity with us and its ongoing implication when it says 'we do not have a high priest who is unable to sympathise with our weaknesses, but we have one who has been tempted in every way, just as we are -yet was without sin' (Heb. 4:15). This is quite astounding when we grasp the reality. The writer of Hebrews is not just talking about the high priesthood of Christ in the future but actually its role at the present time. According to him, our high priest, having offered the perfect sacrifice, is acting on our behalf at this very moment and not only do we have access to him, but the assurance that we shall find 'grace to help us in our time of need'(Heb. 4:16). Yes, as we are exploring in this chapter, there is future glory, but there is also present reality. This concept of Christ's ongoing high priestly ministry is of enormous pastoral and personal use, something that Sir Walter Raleigh discovered some centuries before us.

Some years ago I discovered 'The Passionate Man's Pilgrimage', a poem believed to have been penned by Sir Walter Raleigh as he was about to die, having fallen out of favour with the establishment of his day. As the title suggests, life is depicted as a pilgrimage, one that was coming to a very nasty and tragic end for Sir Walter. In contemplating death and what lies beyond, his mind turns to heaven and a vision of Christ standing there acting on his behalf. It would appear that as he sat in his cell his mind turned

> From thence to heaven's bribeless hall
> Where no corrupted voices brawl,
> No conscience molten into gold,
> Nor forged accusers bought and sold,
> No cause deferred, nor vain-spent journey,
> For there Christ is the King's Attorney,
> Who pleads for all without degrees,
> And he hath angels, but no fees.
> When the grand twelve million jury
> Of our sins with sinful fury
> 'Gainst our souls black verdicts give,
> Christ pleads his death, and then we live.
> Be thou my speaker, taintless pleader,
> Unblotted lawyer, true proceeder;
> Thou movest salvation even for alms,
> Not with a bribed lawyer's palms.

What a graphic depiction of the Lord acting on behalf of us. Having been 'born of a woman, born under the law' (Gal. 4:4), Christ has fully satisfied the demands of the law on our behalf and now stands as our representative. He is the ultimate defence lawyer who secures us the full rights as children of God. He answers every accusation brought against his people and quashes every voice that clamours against us, even those of the skeletons in closet that keep shouting. All that would condemn has been put to death on the cross with Christ. It is to him we point when the evil one raises an accusing finger against us. Sin went to the grave with the Lord but it would not rise again:

only he would do that. By his death and resurrection, Jesus broke the power of Sin and Death in our lives.

Ah, but you say, "I still sin and, unless the Lord returns soon, I shall die". Yes, that is true, but it is only part of the story. We need to step back again and see the whole picture. This is precisely where our friend, whom we left standing on the streets of New York in the last chapter, will be an enormous help. As he had stepped out onto the sidewalk with his new citizenship papers, the objective reality was that he was now under the jurisdiction of a new authority. The nationality that was his by birth had no longer any claim on him. The fact was that he was an American citizen, even though there would be times when subjective feelings would play havoc with his sense of identity. By analogy, the Christian has changed citizenship. Born into a regime where Sin and Death ruled without mercy and exception, the believer is re-born into a whole new order of things. In Christ the old powers are broken and the objective reality is that now life is lived under another Lordship.

However, we need to be very clear that while Sin and Death as dictators have been defeated we are not necessarily free from sins and death as a personal experiences.

Sin and Death	Our sins and our deaths
Universal	Individual
Regimes	Occurrences

In Christ, and in the grand scheme of things, the power of the old tyrants, Sin and Death, has been broken. That is the objective fact. My citizenship papers say I belong to a kingdom where only Christ reigns, but as yet that kingdom is not fully realized. It has started, as we have been emphasizing throughout this book, but it is yet to be consummated. Until it is, I must live in a world where the old regime is still engaged in guerrilla warfare. Ultimately there is victory in Christ, but immediately there is a daily battle. My citizenship states I belong to the *age to come* but my life has to be lived out where *this age* is only too evident. This tension is graphically illustrated by Paul when he addresses the church 'in Corinth' who are also 'in Christ' (1 Cor. 1:2). Our new citizenship changes our status but not necessarily our location. As a Christian, I may have been reborn spiritually into a whole new order of things but I may be required to live in the street where I was born physically. There is not a day that I do not face temptation and engage in a struggle with sins. That the war has been won in Christ gives me no excuse not to fight a daily battle. In him, Sin's strangle hold has been broken but by his Spirit I must wage an ongoing campaign against sins. The waiting room is not a place to sit idle but an arena where real enemies are to be faced down.

Furthermore, it may be helpful to see the parallels between our experience of Sin and *our sins* with Death and *our deaths*. Several years of pastoral ministry and the history of my own family have made me think about my mortality. Without trying to be morbid, for that is not my nature, I am increasingly aware that unless the Lord returns, I shall die and be buried. How is this to be understood in light of the fact that Jesus promises eternal life to his followers? As a Christian, I die with the hope of a resurrection. Yes, my body goes to the grave but with the knowledge that the despot Death has been dethroned. The grave has no ultimate grip. My experience of death as a personal event is real but not final. Christ has been raised from the dead, 'the firstfruits of those who have fallen asleep…so all in Christ will be made alive. But each in his own turn: Christ the firstfruits; then when he comes, those who belong to him' (1 Cor. 15:20-23). We shall return to this in the next section where the resurrected body will be our focus, but for now our aim to establish *our deaths* are not final because Death's regime has been broken by Christ.

Pastorally this is a crucial fact to grasp. Sometimes at gravesides people hear the words read out,

> 'Where O death, is your victory?
> Where, O death, is your sting?' (1Cor. 15:55).

From this, some wrongly deduct from these lines that it is inappropriate for Christians to mourn. These verses are interpreted to mean that true believers are virtually immunized from the sting of the grave. However, here is a striking instance of a verse where context is king. Immediately before these wonderful lines which have been quoted from the prophet Hosea, Paul had just set the time when these words would be applicable. He spoke of when the last trumpet would sound and 'the dead will be raised imperishable, and we will all be changed …*then* the saying that is written will come true: "Death has been swallowed up in victory."'(1 Cor. 15:52-54 emphasis added). He is referring to Christ's return, and it is then, and only then, will Death, 'the last enemy'(1 Cor. 15:26), be destroyed. Until then, people needed room to grieve, but the crucial difference lay in the fact that their mourning was not 'like the rest of men, who have no hope' (1 Thes. 4:13). Believers were to be neither stoical, suppressing all feelings, nor neurotic, giving in to despair. There was, and still is, room for real grief in the waiting room but only because there is real hope beyond it. How Paul used this to bring comfort will become clear in the next section when we look at the resurrection of the body.

In summary, we have seen the human condition in this age was desperate. Christ burst into this tragedy to bear sin, subject himself to law and suffer death for our sake. Now in him the power of that old regime has been broken and human beings may live in a new-found freedom in him. To emphasize the nature of this freedom, we are going to look at how Paul employs the radical image of circumcision and John takes up the idea of a whole new creation.

Circumcision seems a shocking image to be taking up at this stage in a chapter about the heavenly city. Yet, perhaps it is its very shocking nature that arrests our attention and boldly serves the purpose. It is not a topic that is often discussed or preached about in Christian circles yet it was taken up by Paul to give us a rather dramatic perspective on the death of Jesus. Writing to the first-century Colossians, the apostle established the headship of Christ and then said 'in him you were also circumcised, in the putting off of the sinful nature, not with a circumcision done with the hands of men but with the circumcision done by Christ, having been buried with him in baptism and raised with him through your faith in the power of God, who raised him from the dead' (Col. 2:11-12).

Back in Genesis, at the beginning of the story we have been tracing, God commanded Abraham to circumcise his sons. The ceremony, which was administered to an eight-day old boy, involved the ceremonial cutting off a piece of the foreskin as a visible sign of the covenant between God and Israel. Incidentally, it is significant that in the Ancient Near East covenants were 'cut' between parties. The use of this verb immediately conjures up the thought of blood and the solemnity of the occasion. An oath sworn in blood is the highest form of commitment. Every Jewish male wore the sign of the covenant. At eight days old, Jesus, too, would have been circumcised. His parents, who were Torah-observant Jews who would have seen to this, but what they would not have foreseen was an even more radical event when their son would be 'cut off from the land of the living' (Isa. 53:8).

Crucifixion was extreme circumcision. Both circumcision and crucifixion were painfully administered to human flesh. Both inflict pain, draw blood and 'cut off' flesh. Granted there is huge difference between the two on one level but, from the perspective of the point that Paul wants to make, the difference is more quantitative than qualitative. The ritual undergone by Jesus in the first days of his life is symbolic of the reality to be endured in the last days of his life. At this point, it is hard not to be reminded of the experience of Isaac who twice submitted to a knife in the hand of his father Abraham. Firstly, as a boy he received the sign of the covenant but then as a young man he lay bound on an altar as Abraham 'reached out his hand and took the knife to slay his son' (Gen. 22:10). On that occasion the angel of the Lord miraculously intervened and spared the life of Isaac but the symbolism is still powerful. The message seems to have been that Isaac's old life had to be cut off completely, not just symbolically, before he could enter into the full blessings of the covenant promises given to his father.

When Jesus hung on the cross there was no intervention from the angel. He died, and moreover, in him, 'we died to sin' (Rom. 6:2). Paul affirms 'we know that our old self was crucified with him so that the body of sin might be done away with, that we should not longer be slaves to sin – because anyone who has died has been freed from sin' (Rom. 6:6). The totalitarian regimes of Sin and Death have been broken once and for all time. This was the dramatic message given to the Colossian believers, that 'in him you were also circumcised, in the putting off of your sinful nature, not with a circumcision done by the hands of men but with the circumcision done by Christ' (Col. 2:11). This is still the liberating message of the gospel. Not only has the believer been given a new citizenship, but has been effectively 'cut off' from the old way of living. When God's plan is complete, that old order will have gone completely and there will be a new creation.

For the sake of clarity, let's take one last look at our triangles

Acts of creation begin and end our Bibles. As Genesis records the first order of creation so Revelation concludes with John's vision of 'a new heaven and a new earth, for the first heaven and the first earth had passed away' (Rev. 21:1). John opens a door into the heavenly throne room where God is

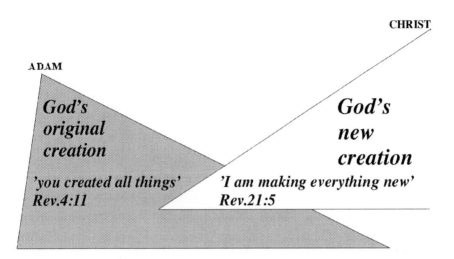

praised as the creator of '*all things*' (Rev. 4:11). He then concludes with an announcement from the throne itself as God declares, "'I am making everything new!'" (Rev. 21:5). The New Jerusalem is part of this new genesis. In this new creation there will be no place for mortality, suffering or evil. Now the words of Isaiah ring out as never before. 'Forget the former things; do not dwell in the past. See, I am doing a new thing!' (Isa.43:19). Moreover, what will be true of creation as a whole will also be true of the individual in particular. Citizens of the new city will have new bodies.

No more pain – the body is now transformed

Sometimes, poetry is a better vehicle than prose when trying to share such stupendous things as we have been exploring. What we are about to survey was once condensed into a few stunning lines by the Jesuit poet, Gerard Manley Hopkins who, anticipating the transformation at the resurrection of our bodies, said,

Enough! the Resurrection,
A heart's-clarion! Away grief's gasping, ' joyless days, dejection.
Across my foundering deck shone
A beacon, an eternal beam. ' Flesh fade, and mortal trash
Fall to the residuary worm; ' world's wildfire, leave but ash:

In a flash, at a trumpet crash,
I am all at once what Christ is, ' since he was what I am, and
This Jack, joke, poor potsherd, ' patch, matchwood, immortal diamond,
Is immortal diamond.

(THAT NATURE IS A HERACLITAN FIRE AND OF THE COMFORT OF
THE RESURRECTION, G.M.Hopkins)

Hopkins's language has a unique intensity. I sometimes use his poetry in my
private devotions and have discovered that while he is so economical, even
stark, in his use of words, the ones that he does choose bulge with meaning.
He realizes that he is cramming miracles of cosmic proportions into the
language of everyday life. What is more beyond the scope of that mundane
world than the prospect of our bodies being resurrected and glorified? Life in
the new creation is life in a new body.

Now, I have met some Christians who seem to have problems with this idea.
They seem to be a bit unsure of how to relate to their bodies in this world and
actually hope to escape completely from them in the world to come. Some
actually believe that salvation promises the soul an escape from the prison
house of the present physical body. In the sweet bye and bye, the soul will fly
away, leaving the fleshly frame, never to return. However, the future hope
described in the Bible is not about liberation from, but rather transformation
of, the body.

Bodies matter in the Bible. Bodies were created by, and are important to God.
In Christ, God assumed a body. To value the spiritual nature above the
physical nature of a person is to side with Greek philosophy rather than divine
revelation. Nowhere in the Scriptures is there any indication that the physical
side of a human creature was imperfect for the simple reason that it was
material. True enough, the Hebrews were very conscious of the gap between
the creator and the creature, between the world of God and the world of man,
but that gulf was never explained away in terms of humans being inferior
because they were physical and lived in a material world. God had created
both the world and the bodies in which humans lived. All that God made was
good, and that included the material as well as the spiritual. Hebrew thought
knows nothing of that strict dualism that separates body from soul or flesh
from spirit. While these may be irreconcilable opposites to some Greek
philosophers, they are simply two aspects of being human for the Hebrew

writers of Scripture. The Bible presents us as beings who are fully physical and fully spiritual. That Hebraic mindset is evident in the record of the first Christmas when the Spirit overshadowed Mary and the Word became flesh. In Christ there was absolutely no enmity between Spirit and flesh. Moreover, the physical body that left the womb would be raised from the tomb at the other end of his life on earth. There is a distinctively bodily aspect to the Christian hope of resurrection. That means our friend, whom we have introduced in an earlier chapter standing on the streets New York struggling with the tension of objective facts and subjective feelings, will one day have a new body for his life in the new city. This 'new' body will be a transformation, and not a replacement, of his present body. This new one will be part of the new creation, beyond all threat of evil, destruction or any other aspect of mortality. His new citizenship is the beginning of his life in the new creation.

That is what awaits us when the purposes of God are all complete, but once again we need to return to the questions that naturally arise among those of us still in the waiting room. Two of the most often–asked questions are about what happens now after we die and how will our future body relate to our present one. Again, any answer has to wrestle with the fact that we are living in the overlap of two ages. We keep returning to this point, but it is fundamental. This is the wider context that shapes our understanding of things. The *age to come* has been inaugurated but not consummated. Already we have so much, but there is so much more that has not yet come. Like those early believers who lived 'in Corinth' but also 'in Christ', we may have citizenship in the coming kingdom but the reality of the present age is still around us and the last enemy is yet to be finally destroyed. So what does this mean for me if I die before the Lord returns?

Firstly it means an unnatural separation of my body and spirit. We have seen that Hebraic thought allows for no division between the spiritual and physical aspects of a person but my death is an event marked by my body being buried and my spirit going to be with the Lord. Surely we have stood by enough gravesides not to be in any doubt about the former fact, but perhaps we need reminding of the Scriptures which assure us about the latter. Separation from the body does not mean separation from the Lord. Paul recognised the reality of this when he said that he 'would prefer to be away from the body and at home with the Lord' (2 Cor. 5:8). He affirmed to the Philippians that his death meant going to 'be with Christ' (Phil. 1:23). Moreover, there was an immediacy to the promise of the crucified Lord, who promised the thief on his dying day, 'you will be with me in Paradise' (Luke 23:43). The Book of Hebrews refers to 'the spirits of just men made perfect' (Heb. 12:22) being in the heavenly gathering.

Yet, while clearly affirming the presence of the saints with their Lord, the Scriptures and our experience teach us that the bodies lie in the grave. The last enemy of this age still has a disruptive power. Obviously, the higher our conception of the unity of the person, then the greater will be our urgency to see this period come to an end. However, until the Lord comes in glory the body must lie in the grave. It lies in the grave like a seed planted in the earth. Paradoxically the seed decays before it bursts into life. Every Christian burial is like a planting. There is the expectation that what has gone into the ground will not be buried for ever. The cold clay and the headstone seem to defy such a belief but already their hold on the dead has been broken. Our confidence lies in the fact that already 'Christ has been raised from the dead, the *firstfruits* of those who have fallen asleep' (1 Cor. 15:20 emphasis added).

The term 'firstfruits' is not new to us. We met the word in the last chapter where it was used of the coming of the Holy Spirit. It is primarily an agricultural term designating the beginning of the crop. Every farmer understood the firstfruits as the first of a kind, the first of many, the first that guaranteed more of the same. How eminently appropriate it was as an image to comfort grieving Corinthians. Perhaps Paul stood with them in the local cemetery. It just seemed nothing had or ever would happen there. It was literally a dead end. However, into this despair and disappointment, Paul the pastor, brought hope. He pointed to the ground and affirmed that from it Christ has already risen, the firstfruits who guarantees that there is a greater resurrection to follow. 'But each in his own turn: Christ the firstfruits; then when he comes, those who belong to him' (1 Cor. 15:23). As we have said so often before, the Christ event was only the beginning of the end. We are still waiting the climax.

While this is the greatest of hopes, there were those in Corinth, as there are some today, who ask '" How are the dead raised? With what kind of body will they come?"' (1 Cor. 15:35). We find that, as with creation so with the individual body, the emphasis is on renewal not replacement. God, as the creator of everything, has the power to make all things new again and put them beyond all threat of evil or destruction. Suffering and mortality are not in the nature of this new body that will be fitted for eternity. However, the natural question we ask is how does this 'new' body relate to our present one. I would like to suggest an analogy to help us explore this extraordinary reality. In many ways the relationship between the old and new bodies is like that between Old and New Testaments. Firstly there is a clear element of continuity between the two. Features found in the old are readily traceable to, and identifiable in, the new. However, secondly, within this very continuity there is often a marked element of contrast. What lies at the heart of that contrast is the fact that what we encounter in the new is simply superior to anything that had been before. So any reflection on the heavenly body must take seriously these three elements of continuity, contrast and superiority. The same three elements come into play when we think on the relationship between the oak tree and the acorn or the horse chestnut tree and the conker. Without denying the continuity, Paul does major on the contrasting superiority of the new body when he says 'the dead will be raised imperishable, and we will be changed. For the perishable must clothe itself with the imperishable, and the mortal with immortality. When the perishable has been clothed with the imperishable, and the mortal with immortality, then the saying that is written will come true: "Death has been swallowed up in victory"'. (1Cor. 15:53).

In the meantime death still has its sting. However, from the perspective we have been taking, we see that at the moment Death can only engage in a series of smash and grab raids. While it bursts in on life and snatches people away, its grasp is limited. The clutches of Death have been broken, Christ, the firstfruits, is the evidence of that and in time the last enemy will disappear totally. There will be no more separation. Bodies and spirits, divided by death, will be reunited and glorified for life in the new creation. There will be wholeness.

No more brokenness – shalom is now everywhere.

Since beginning this journey together we have discovered a number of words that have suffered verbal inflation. Like the money in the our pockets they just do not go as far as they used to. 'Shalom' is another of these words. Popular on greetings cards, the term has been reduced to meaning 'peace' but that is a serious devaluation of the original. To trace the family tree of the word is to discover that its roots were in the realm of wholeness or completeness. So this term does more than denote the absence of strife or war. Rather in a positive way it designates health, well being, an internal condition of being at ease and fulfilment. In short, it is really the condition that God intends humanity to live. In the new creation, shalom will not just be a sentiment on a greetings card but it will be the very nature of life itself.

Jews still greet each other by asking "How is your shalom?". In other words, "How are you? Are you complete today?" In the new creation shalom will be the way of living. In the lives of the people and on the streets of the new city there will be shalom. The city that will come down from above will be radically different from any city that we can imagine. The Babel that we visited in the first chapter is closer to what we call a city. There we discovered the very antithesis of the garden. The human quest for identity, security, solidarity and permanence in the city backfired producing loneliness, fear and uncertainty. However, the strange irony is that the closing chapters of Revelation return to the theme of the city as the New Jerusalem descends. John 'saw the Holy City, the new Jerusalem, coming down out of heaven from God, prepared as a bride beautifully dressed for her husband' (Rev. 21:2).Where once the city had been the human attempt to divorce everyday life from God, now the city has become his bride. Where human autonomy had driven a wedge between creator and creature, now a divine initiative had restored the intimacy. Incidentally, I wonder if like me you are struck by the downward movement in John's vision of the end. So often when people talk about the end of the world as we know it the movement of their thinking is upward and away from the earth. A careful reading of Revelation reverses that tendency as the picture there is of God coming down. In fact that has been a striking feature of his activity throughout our study, as he came down to the garden, tent and temple. He came down in the flesh to the level of the humanity he came to save and he has come down in the Spirit. Perhaps that thought may serve as a corrective to those escapist eschatologies that have become all too rampant.

Inside the city that comes down, there awaits an even greater surprise. The garden is restored! 'Then the angel showed me the river of the water of life, as clear as crystal, flowing from the throne of God and of the Lamb down the middle of the great street of the city. On each side of the river stood the tree

of life, bearing twelve crops of fruit, yielding its fruit every month'
(Rev. 22:1-2). Where once the city had been the arch enemy of the garden, we
now find them reconciled. At what price? Only Christ who sweated blood in
the Garden of Gethsemane and who died outside the city walls of Jerusalem
could answer that. His perfect work brings wholeness to both the city and its
citizens. If the garden surprises us by its presence then perhaps the temple
surprises us by its absence.

No more temple – the presence is now perfect.

The most holy room in the structure where the Glory-Presence came to earth
was known as the Holy of Holies or the Most Holy. Always a perfect cube,
this inner sanctuary is a fascinating place to enter. Of course there was no
image or earthly representation of the Lord but the outspread wings of the
cherubim bespoke his presence. In my imagination I sometimes stand in this
awesome room and let my mind follow what I like to call 'the cube route'.
That route starts in the Tent of Meeting in the wilderness. Take a moment as
you read and join me in this innermost room at the western end of the
structure. To enter we shall walk along an east – west axis, the most holy
room always standing at the western end. Commencing at the eastern gateway
we shall traverse the courtyard, pass the washbasin, and enter the outer room
with its symbolic furniture. Then comes that special moment as we pass
through the veil into the very presence of the Almighty. We are confronted
with the outspread wings of two cherubim. Back in Genesis two such
cherubim wielding swords had stood guarding the eastern gate to Eden. Their
presence barred Adam and Eve from re-entering the garden after their
expulsion. Now the swords are gone and the gates have been opened. Access
to the Almighty is now possible thanks to his own initiative. This inner
sanctum of the tent is a perfect cube, fifteen feet by fifteen feet by fifteen feet
(Exod. 26:31-35). Normally only the great High Priest would dare to enter on
the Day of Atonement but we can enter through the mind's eye. The perfect
cube is resplendent. The walls are gilt and the only furniture is the Ark of the
Covenant with the cherubim poised on the lid.

Close your eyes for a moment as we travel to the time of King Solomon. Open
them again to find ourselves still in Most Holy Place but now surrounded by
the temple. While our feet stand squarely on the solid floor and we are

surrounded by permanent stone walls, but the room is somewhat larger, now about thirty feet by thirty feet by thirty feet (1 Kgs. 6:19). We are further along the 'cube route' but the most exciting leap is yet to come. From the Jerusalem stone of Solomon's city our mental trajectory takes us to the New Jerusalem of John's great final vision. Stand in awe as we watch this gargantuan city come down from above. It is overwhelming! It is a perfect cube!

Both the tent and the temple had been nothing more than prototypes. On a micro scale they introduced what would ultimately be revealed on the macro scale of the New Jerusalem. As that city is revealed, so the promise given to slaves being liberated from Egypt will be fulfilled. 'Now the dwelling of God is with men, and he will live with them and be their God. He will wipe every tear from their eyes. There will be no more death or mourning or crying or pain, for the old order of things has passed away' (Rev. 21:3-4)

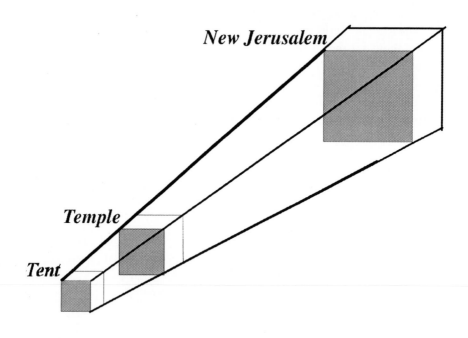